Richard Kislan is a professor of speech, theater, and dance at Glassboro State College, New Jersey, where he researches, lectures, directs campus theatrical productions, and conducts workshops on the American musical theater. He received his M.A. and Ph.D. from New York University. His experience with musicals during the last two decades include engagements as a singer, dancer, actor, director, choreographer, rehearsal pianist, composer, and lyricist.

THE MUSICAL

A Look at the American Musical Theater

RICHARD KISLAN

A SPECTRUM BOOK

PRENTICE-HALL, INC., Englewood Cliffs, N.J. 07632

Library of Congress Cataloging in Publication Data

Kislan, Richard.
   The musical.

   (A Spectrum Book)
   Includes index.
   1. Musical revue, comedy, etc.—United States—
History and criticism. I. Title.
ML1711.K57   782.8'1'0973   79–25762
ISBN 0–13–608547–4
ISBN 0–13–608539–3 pbk.

A SPECTRUM BOOK

Printed in the United States of America

10 9 8 7 6 5 4 3 2

Editorial/production supervision and interior design by Maria Carella.
Cover design by Judith Kazdym Leeds.
Manufacturing buyer: Cathie Lenard.

*Cover photograph by Martha Swope Photography, Inc.,
New York, New York*

PRENTICE-HALL INTERNATIONAL, INC., *London*
PRENTICE-HALL OF AUSTRALIA PTY., LIMITED, *Sydney*
PRENTICE-HALL OF CANADA, LTD., *Toronto*
PRENTICE-HALL OF INDIA PRIVATE, LIMITED, *New Delhi*
PRENTICE-HALL OF JAPAN, INC., *Tokyo*
PRENTICE-HALL OF SOUTHEAST ASIA PTE., LTD., *Singapore*
WHITEHALL BOOKS, LIMITED, *Wellington, New Zealand*

CONTENTS

FORMS
OF MUSICAL THEATER

v

THE
MATURE MUSICAL

ELEMENTS
OF MUSICAL THEATER

PREFACE

I wrote this book for anyone who enjoys musical theater. It is a simple book, a book of fundamentals designed for the beginner. It brings together three subjects in one volume: 1) the historical evolution of musical theater forms in America; 2) the ideas, practices and contributions of the mature musical's most influential creative artists; and 3) the major elements of a musical show. The American musical theater is as much a synthesis of these types of information as a musical show is a synthesis of the contributions of many collaborators. As each artist's work develops alone, only to complement that of others in the finished product, so do history, biography, and analysis complement each other in the American musical theater tradition. The tripartite structure of this book reflects that premise.

The United States is a young nation with an old musical theater tradition. Since 1735, the American musical has been alive and growing, assimilating and rejecting, evolving and achieving. Forms appear, disappear, reappear. Distinguished veterans establish rules; talented newcomers break them. Critics submit periodical obituaries, but the musical refuses to die.

Since few phenomena avoid formula as resolutely as does the American musical theater tradition, I make no attempt to suggest a theory, much less advance an argument for the predictable linear descent of the modern musical from some archetypal form. I hope only to enlighten the reader with a simple narrative, one that reflects in tone and manner the character of its subject.

Unfortunately, space considerations demand the regrettable omission of certain forms, personalities, and achievements. Since the book is intended only as an introduction to its subject, it is hoped that any questioned exclusions stimulate the reader to research the subject further.

Part One surveys the variety of foreign and domestic musical theater forms evident in the United States from the colonial period to the twentieth century. If by musical theater we mean a staged dramatic entertainment in which music is used as a vital creative component, then it is not hyperbole to suggest that America always had a musical theater. When the evolution of forms stabilized, as it did in the early twentieth century, the focus of the book shifts to the ideas of important creative artists who committed their talent and craft to perfecting practices within the inherited forms.

Part Two deals with the considerable artistic influence of writers, composers and lyricists whose achievements carried the American musical from early potential to recognized achievement. These artists created and sustained the "mature musical," one that takes itself seriously as art as well as entertainment, and promotes dramatic and theatrical standards that withstand comparison to serious drama. While popular songwriters like Irving Berlin, Cole Porter, George Gershwin, and Lerner and Loewe contributed much to the twentieth-century musical, it was Jerome Kern, Rodgers and Hammerstein, and Stephen Sondheim who set the ship of tradition to sail in significant new directions. That the American musical matured into impressive art and big business is due to these talented and dedicated people.

Part Three describes the basic elements of a musical show: book, lyrics, score, dance, and design. Musical theater is the most collaborative of all the arts. An audience that is prepared to recognize and understand each part is more apt to appreciate the highly complex system of a finished show.

As an introductory survey committed to a simple overview of a complex and far-ranging tradition, this book admits to many of the liabilities of its type: necessary omissions, frequent generalizations, and superficial treatment. In addition, I am aware that some of the question- **viii** able judgments and provocative conclusions in the introductory chapter entitled "A Philosophy of Musical Theater" may provoke controversy. I chose to begin the book with a personal statement of what the musical theater appears to be in the majority of cases because no serious subject operates completely outside the framework of the theories and ideas we call its philosophy. Should you disagree with this approach, its method or conclusions, let that be a starting point to your self-education in the field. The world of the American musical theater is an open society mature enough to withstand artistic quarrels. Audiences are the lifeblood of the theater, and *we* are that audience. It matters less that we disagree, than that through argument, research, and participation, we continue to care.

In our time, the American musical has become a source of achievement in the arts by giving its considerable audience an experience that director-choreographer Bob Fosse described as an evening in the theater when "everybody has a good time—even in the crying scenes." I hope this book gives everybody a good time, reawakens the joy of remembered musicals and leads to a more enlightened appreciation of this popular American art.

RICHARD KISLAN
Brigantine, New Jersey

INTRODUCTION: A PHILOSOPHY OF MUSICAL THEATER

Musical theater acknowledges a history as old as history itself. Our Paleolithic ancestors chanted prescribed rituals in dark inaccessible places long before language, records, logic, or systems. While scholarly speculation about that primitive theater of ritual tempts us to infer conclusions about mankind's archetypal disposition to a lyric theater, the idea of the musical theater as we know it begins much later with the deliberate union of drama and song in opera. From the moment in the late Renaissance when Florentine students developed a viable musical drama, audiences have enjoyed such alternatives to the spoken drama as operetta, ballet, pantomime, minstrelsy, vaudeville, burlesque, extravaganza, revue, musical comedy, and musical play. Different as these forms may be in content, structure, and origin, each shares basic assumptions about what the art of the theater should be. To recognize these principles is to acknowledge a philosophy of musical theater. To accept them is to believe in it.

All musical theater embodies the spirit and philosophy of the *theater of romance*. Life is the stuff of all drama, but while the theater of realism presents the unadorned truth of life as it is, the theater of romance presents life as it should be. When artists of the theater make the average, the ordinary, and the everyday give way to the special, the unique, and the exceptional, the theater becomes a shelter for unfettered imagination put to the service of life's affirmation and celebration. Here, man can aspire to be more than himself. He can quest and adventure, risk and achieve. Integrity reigns in a kingdom 2 of values and dreams, bravery and sacrifice. As the romantic poets of the nineteenth century fled their domestic environment into distant lands filled with imagined giants and exotic causes, so does the romantic theater reject the limitations of the ordinary for a self-made world of sublime and moral art. Here, intellectual attitudes give way to emotion, passion prevails over decorum, and above all, romantic love radiates from the center of all things.

The concept of romantic love originated in the Middle Ages when the troubadours of Provence put unsatisfied desire into their poetic conception of love, thereby forging a new ideal capable of embodying all of man's purest moral and social aspirations without totally sacrificing the more sensual alternatives. Romantic love meant ideal love: selfless, spiritual, eternal. When represented in the medieval images of the knight-champion and the knight-lover, love became the energy for heroism, the argument for fidelity, and the heart and soul of chivalry. Time has not diminished the power of this ideal to inspire man to reach out beyond realistic limitation, because the romantic vision celebrates forever the wonder of living. It endows its adherents with an emotional ascendency not unlike feeling the weight of mortality melt away while knowing one is mortal still. If man admits to the need for this deeply felt emotional experience that carries all before it, then man allows the cause for a musical theater.

Why a musical theater? Simply, song and dance in the service of romantic ideals exclude all other alternatives. People do not behave in real life as they are made to do in a musical show because song raises the listener and the singer to a higher artistic level than does ordinary speech. Song invests its ideas with a radiant emotional power that gives sentiment the wings to soar above reality. Song recalls in the listener personal experiences of deep and highly charged feeling, permitting an audience to feel together what has been felt before alone. Is there one of us who has never been attached to a song? Remember? It was an attachment so deep and true because that all-enveloping song somehow sprang from life's experiences and yet managed to transcend them. Song enriches
3 human life by raising the ordinary to the exceptional,

thereby making it more real than real. When song becomes the inevitable and appropriate tool for transmitting the full range of dramatic ideas, it achieves a musical theater of overwhelming artifice subject to the passionate adoration of adherents as well as the serious objections of critics who resist a form they see only as a juvenile and perverse retreat from the realities of life. Do the facts of a life distinguish it as much as how we feel about them, or more appropriately, how we feel about each other? Romantic artists have always pursued a reality beyond what appears to the senses. What was most real was felt, and so passed on as a transformation of what was seen and heard. So does the musical theater transform and recreate, thus providing audiences with an alternative approach to the dramatization of the mysteries and contradictions of human experience.

Musical theater is *total theater*, an artistic system that not only encourages the use of techniques beyond the spoken word for projecting dramatic ideas but makes nonliteral dramatic revelation a priority in the creative and interpretative process. Musical theater is the most collaborative form in all the arts. To measure a work accurately means to weigh the contributions of librettist, composer, lyricist, director, choreographer, actors, singers, dancers, and designers of scenery, costume, and lighting. Note: (1) each component is essential to the composition of the whole, and (2) the majority involve arts and skills that are nonverbal. Fundamentally, musical theater offers an intricate and colorful puzzle for the senses with each piece complete enough in its artistry to fulfill a prescribed function while subservient enough to submit to the assimilation necessary for the total effect of a work that in performance loses, as if by magic, the seams that separate the parts. An effective musical is always greater than the sum of its parts. A song in such a show achieves status beyond that of highlight of a scene because it becomes the scene, its essence, its purpose, its drama. Total theater pursues extraordinary objectives through a total assault on the senses, opening up to the audience the grandest avenues of sound, color, and movement. Artifice, no doubt, but splendid artifice, capable of accumulating a power of performance characteristically grand, enveloping, and total.   **4**

Musical theater is *moral art* in that it is life-affirming in content and process, thus conforming to the argument for moral direction in the arts that John Gardner advances in his book *On Moral Fiction.* The sublime message of any musical show must ultimately be: life is worth it. Even when things do not turn out all right in the end, the very existence of the artifact which is the show inspires hope, promotes growth, and reaffirms life. The cynicism and despair that inhibit human and artistic development are anathema to musical theater. Has not the lesson of Rodgers and Hammerstein been that the skilled integration of musical-dramatic elements that reveal optimistic content promotes consistent success in the popular musical theater? To dismiss their work as the naïve statement of old-fashioned moralists is to overlook how well their point of view matched the moral theater they chose to work in.

The process of musical theater is life-affirming as well. Identify the principal tools of its craftsmen. Movement. Song. Dance. Each distinguishes moments when we are truly alive. Do men have any greater sense of life's opportunity as when they thrust their bodies into space? Ask the runner. Ask the invalid. What is dance if not the vocabulary and grammar of life's actions given form? What is song if not the internal movement of mind and emotion externalized in sound. As human activity, each points out the presence of life. As art, each celebrates it. Since great art not only mirrors but shapes a culture, we must not underestimate the impact of musical theater as a popular and subtle force in the argument for moral direction in an increasingly confused and impolite world.

Musical theater is a *popular theater*, entertainment created by and for the majority of average people. The political ideal of democracy advanced in a classless society has allowed entertainment since the early nineteenth century to speak to and for the mass audience and not just the elite few. A popular theater emerged, but not without liabilities like the hallmark tendency to exploit the plain, the familiar, the cheap, and the vulgar. Nevertheless, all great and prolific periods in theater history were periods of popular theater, and the American musical theater is nothing if not prolific. Today, it is popular, too, with the annual production of Broadway musicals arousing the interest and potential support of so many that its activity has become an enormous commercial enterprise. Quantitative measures exist to confirm popularity and success, notably, long runs, box-office receipts, film sales, original cast albums, and media spinoffs. Yet commercial success reflects popularity, it doesn't explain it. The vitality of the contemporary musical theater comes from a noncommercial source—the continuous recognition by generations of audiences that the materials, forms, and styles of the musical developed out of lessons learned from the intimate relationship a musical show establishes with its live and responsive public. A musical theater is a theater of the people. It gives to an audience, but takes from it, too.

Anyone who has ever played or created for the musical stage knows (or soon learns) that all musical theater is *presentational.* The cumulative impact of live singing, dancing, acting, and musical accompaniment reminds the audience and the performers throughout of the vigorous theatricality of the event. This presentational nature evolved from exposure to consistent audience reaction and applause generated by song, dance, and scenic effects. A musical not only welcomes a spontaneous and displayed audience reaction, but builds for it, thrives on it, and learns from it. Presentationalism means more than a style of presentation. Presentationalism defines the dominant creative and interpretative philosophy which accounts for the unique nature of musical theater as art. For example, the presentational value of the musical theater book rests not so much on considerations of story, plot shape, or balance, but on the book's potential as catalyst for the total presentational opportunities in the show's idea. If presenting a theatrical idea through music and dance is not significantly different and more theatrically effective than presenting an idea without it, there is no point in creating a musical at all. Either present the musical or drop the project altogether.

Finally, musical theater requires a strict acceptance of the *conventions* unique to it. All musicals must fail if the audience refuses to accept song as a conventional mode of human expression. Accepting this convention **6** can be difficult at first. The rhythm of singing is slower than that of the spoken language. The tonal range of a song exceeds that of most spoken speech. The melodic profile of a song can make uncomfortable demands on an ear accustomed only to the more natural and acceptable melody of the speaking voice. However, once an audience accepts the conventions of song, they are free to respond not just to the words of a character, but to the rich subtext of secret thoughts, feelings, moods, and attitudes suggested by the music.

It has been said that great art should express for us what we have experienced but are unable to express effectively ourselves. If anything, the history of musical theater in America has been an uninterrupted march toward the crafts that particularize experiences in sound and movement so popular and so universal as to make the American musical the nation's most visible modern contribution to world theater.

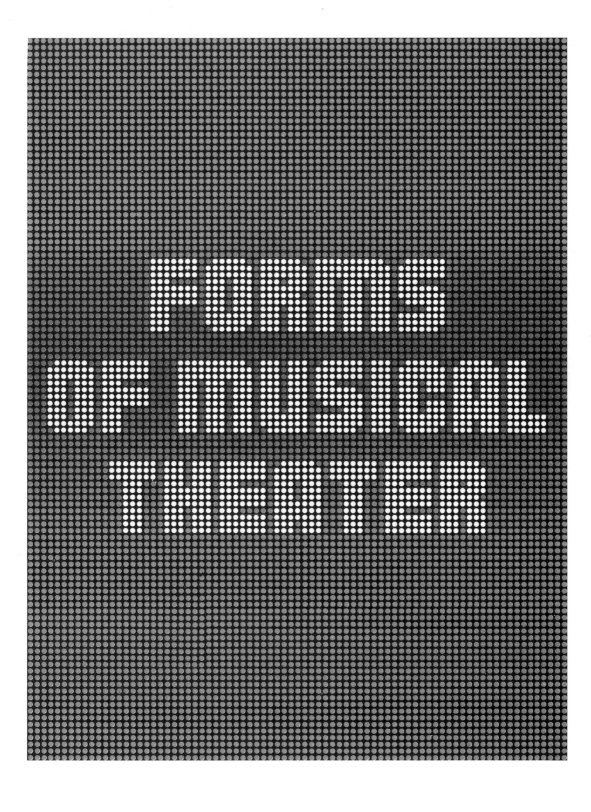

1

EUROPEAN FORMS IN EARLY AMERICA

European forms dominated musical theater activity in colonial America. After all, the colonists inherited from England not only language and custom, but sophisticated tastes in art, architecture, the decorative arts, and theater entertainments. Although importation declined when native talent emerged, the earliest work of the American artists was never less than European in form, style, and spirit. Since the first recorded musical theater performance in the colonies was of a ballad opera, *Flora* (1735), presented without stage, scenery, costumes, or footlights in a courtroom in Charleston, South Carolina, American audiences were given early opportunity to accept the fashionably close interaction between drama and music that dominated the European stage entertainments of the period. Other factors facilitated that interaction. Orchestral concerts in the colonies favored programs of ensemble accompaniment for vocal music derived from opera and oratorios. Many concerts in rural America were initiated and performed by members of touring theatrical companies who were in a very real sense the earliest and most visible American orchestras. Dancing and dancers added still another link between music and theater. As in most cultures, the dances of the colonists made their way onto the stage, and thereafter, what was danced on the stage influenced what was danced at social gatherings. Often, the teachers who taught the dances were the performers associated with the musical stage. Puppet shows, popular in America from the time of the earliest settlements, provided the professional acting companies with the mechanism for demonstrating to an audience the singular character of a musical drama even under the most primitive circumstances. While the puppet show repertory included straight plays with occasional songs between scenes, many of the most popular offerings were musical dramas like the ballad opera, *The Poor Soldier*, a particular audience favorite.

The companies that toured early America recognized and responded to its audiences' growing inclination to a musical stage. Singers and dancers comprised a segment of influence in every troupe, and well-known serious actors were under contract often for their demonstrated ability to fit into a musical drama cast. In the Old America Company, the earliest and most distinguished theater repertory company in colonial America, many of the noted actors were featured singers and dancers as well as distinguished actors. These performers were the undisputed superstars of the period, performers who honored custom by entertaining the audience with songs and dances between the acts of serious and musical plays. Later, these interludes came to be known as "olios"— not to be confused with another form of recognition of audience affection for musical entertainment, the "afterpiece," a distinct musical offering added to the evening's entertainment after the completion of the scheduled performance. Although the "olio" originated as a practical response to some technical problem like diverting the attention of the audience while stagehands shifted cumbersome scenery, the public so enjoyed and demanded these interludes that the custom persisted until late in the nineteenth century when the severe and disciplined theater practices associated with the theater of realism washed away all entertainment excesses in a tidal wave of reform. Before that, however, the musical interludes and those who performed them exerted considerable impact on the young and developing culture. Much like the medieval minstrels before them, these talented and versatile performers wandered through town and country bearing their art and the news of the day to communities eager for the twin amusements of gossip and entertainment. Welcomed, appreciated, honored, they made a place for themselves and their wares in a society even **12** then a fertile market for music, drama, song, and dance. Eventually, touring companies designed the repertory to respond to the tastes of the rapidly developing American audience. The Old America Company featured fifty to sixty musicals as well as a similar number of dramatic plays from 1787 to 1792. Popular enthusiasm for musical stage forms from 1793 to 1800 caused that repertory to expand to about 120 musical stage entertainments. Beyond a doubt, ballad opera was the most popular form.

The Ballad Opera

The ballad opera is not a true opera. Traditionally, the word *opera* defines a dramatic theater piece with continuous music as the dominant artistic feature. In other words, an opera is a play sung entirely to original music created by the composer to extend the dramatic values in the libretto. Nevertheless, it was customary in eighteenth-century England to apply the name *opera* to almost any dramatic work with dialogue and music. Where early opera uses recitative between arias (recitative being the early operatic technique of heightened intoned speech that follows the inflection and rhythm of words set to definite notes and accompanied by specific chords), the ballad opera uses spoken dialogue. Although the ballad opera permitted composers to use new music, the more characteristic procedure was to set new lyrics to old and familiar tunes, usually the popular ballads, airs, and folk songs of the day. Like the Greek tragedies whose plot and background were known already to ancient audiences, the ballad opera capitalized on the effect of material long familiar to its audience. As it favored simple songs, music of easy melody set off by uncomplicated harmonies, its appeal was direct and emotional, much like the appeal of a popular air in the repertory of an eighteenth-century street singer. Since the contemporary definition of *ballad* was "a song commonly sung up and down the street," and since the ballads were the very
13   tunes borrowed for the ballad opera score, the form itself

came to be known as the ballad opera. Although the creator of ballad opera integrated a generous number of songs into the play, music was not permitted to dominate the text. That contemporary audiences who were suffering through incredible florid operas or pallid, sentimental comedies were able once more to respond with vigorous enthusiasm to an acceptable musical drama was due to the spectacular achievement in 1728 of John Gay's *Beggar's Opera.*

"THE BEGGAR'S OPERA"

Not only did *The Beggar's Opera* set the standards, form, and style for all ballad opera, it proved to be the single most popular theatrical work of the eighteenth century—a work so successful that it occupied an important place in the repertory of every theatrical company performing in the colonies during the colonial period. Why? In 1728, John Gay gambled with new ideas about musical theater content and form—and won. He offered a sophisticated public a broad and biting satire on the social and political corruption of England in a theater form that was itself a travesty on the fashionable Italian opera. *The Beggar's Opera* had a strong book, filled with ideas to engage the brain, situations to touch the heart, and diction to approximate the sound of the speaking voice. In addition, it commanded the unintended but not unwelcome notoriety of a "shocking" event, a work filled with satirical intentions but peopled with characters of common and unsavory vices whose behavior dramatizes some unwelcome similarities between the then rigidly segregated social classes. This was the special point of the work: crime is less an affront in a world of poverty than is official corruption. When thieves and whores were made to affect the attitudes and behavior of lords and ladies, the audience could not escape the conclusion that all men were alike in a world that is all the same. The book brought the audience together and made them dramatically aware of a shared humanity. However, not all in the audience saw satire and universality. Some preferred to see only the thieves and the whores. The violent allegations that **14**

The Beggar's Opera was "corrupting the nation's morals" only added to the work's popularity and success.

In addition to a distinguished book, the work offered a unique form that functioned as an effective framework for song. John Gay chose the three-act division rather than the one or two acts of farce or the customary five acts of traditional comedy. Did he sense how well his slight but carefully constructed plot would service the score when structured more as opera than play? Or was he forced by the sheer volume of music, some sixty-nine songs, to consider a form traditional to musical theater? When Gay selected the tunes originally, he intended that they be sung without accompaniment. When the producer of the original production suggested an orchestral component, Johann Christoph Pepusch was engaged to compose an overture and devise the orchestrations. Although the final musical "score" expanded much beyond the author's original intent, the book was never overwhelmed. The musical theater learned a simple lesson: the book comes first.

Comic Opera

Audiences in the colonies favored comic opera as well, so the touring companies included works from the French, Italian, and English repertory. The term *comic opera* stands for a dramatic work on a light or sentimental subject with a considerable amount of music, comedy, and a happy ending. The comic operas of the English tradition contained spoken dialogue rather than recitative, and resembled the French *opéra bouffe* and the German *operetta* in spirit and temperament. However, one major distinction did prevail. The English comic opera emphasized comedy over romance and sentimentality. Its music was an asset in the New World because English composers worked in styles familiar to American audiences. The English comic opera appealed to the theatrical companies, too. Comic opera with dialogue instead of recitative called for good actors, and that, rather than major vocal talent, was a commodity the touring companies could supply.

Pasticcio

An intermediate form between ballad opera and comic opera was the *pasticcio*, a dramatic work for which the writer, producer, or arranger selected music from the compositions of famous composers in order to win over the audience with a distinguished and popular musical program. What appears to be a most unethical practice was quite the proper and popular thing to do in the eighteenth century. Remember, *The Beggar's Opera* was a *pasticcio*, its score adapted from numerous contemporary sources.

Among the lesser European musical theater forms to win an audience in early America were the following: (1) The *burletta*, a burlesque comic opera in three acts with at least five songs, which usually deals in a ludicrous way with classic subjects, legend, or history. Contemporary accounts refer to the form as a "drama in rhyme which is musical" and which emerges in performance as "a poor relation to an opera." (2) Shadow shows, a form of puppetry entertainment in which figures were manipulated between a strong light and a translucent screen. (3) Pantomimes, staged ballets on subjects derived from classical mythology, the commedia dell'arte, or fantastical subjects. (4) Masques, dramatic entertainments in verse on mythical or allegorical subjects with dialogue subordinate to musical spectacle.

For the duration of the eighteenth century, the predominantly upper-class American audience supported a musical theater that was European in origin, form, and style. That was soon to change. As American cities swelled to accommodate great concentrations of common people after the War of 1812, theater activity responded to the new and potentially vast audience with entertainment **16**

Tom and Jerry.

Green. I'll give him a few words of advice.

Act III. Scene 3.

European forms dominated the early American musical stage. A lithograph from an early edition of the burletta *Tom and Jerry*. (Photo: Theatre Collection, Free Library of Philadelphia)

less attuned to the inherited traditions of the past than the burgeoning demands of the present. The stage was set for the development of a musical theater more appropriate to the stuff and style of America.

17

2

MINSTRELSY

The musical theater in America became an American musical theater when exclusive dependence on European models ended with the emergence of minstrelsy, vaudeville, burlesque, spectacle, and extravaganza. To the musical entertainments already common on the stage in the nineteenth century, these indigenous forms added shows of American origin that reflected the character, will, and taste of the American public. Without question, the earliest and most influential form was the minstrel show.

The most popular form of entertainment in the United States during the middle decades of the nineteenth century was the minstrel show, a crude, low-grade style of song, dance, and comedy entertainment more important for what it did than for what it was. Minstrelsy was the impersonation of Negro life and manners by white men in blackface. It developed spontaneously out of the American scene during a time when slavery was an unavoidable fact and a burning issue. The economics of slavery sustained a way of life in one-half of the United States while at the same time the question of its indefensible morality outraged the other half. Minstrelsy evolved into a dominant force in the popular culture of the nation only because it fashioned a romantic and sentimental recreation of a plantation experience that never existed. The music, songs, dances, and comic chatter reflected the public's idealized and stereotyped version of an exotic world floating in a lighthearted atmosphere of plaintive melodies and spontaneous dances. Since the truth would only provoke anxiety, danger, and war, the stereotypes

19

persisted. If minstrelsy commands our attention, it is for native origins, innovative practices, an influential format, and creative artists. Minstrelsy was the first form of American stage entertainment to commission popular music specifically for the stage. The format of the minstrel show inspired the later development of other types of musicals, namely vaudeville, burlesque, and revue. Minstrelsy initiated in America the idea and practice of big-time show business. Charging only twenty-five cents admission, the Christy Minstrels grossed the sum of $317,598 for a single run of a minstrel program. Minstrelsy planted American seeds in American soil for the first time in musical theater history. What grew was strong, if not pretty—the hardy stock on which later generations of theatrical artists would graft the colorful hybrids that bloomed late into the twentieth century.

Origins

Blackface entertainment itself did not originate in the United States. The phallophoroi of the ancient Greek theater, Renaissance Moors, and the Pulcinella and Arlecchino of the commedia dell'arte represent earlier manifestations. Although performers in the American colonies during the eighteenth century inserted select Negro dances or Negro caricature in song between the acts of plays and operas, blackface *acts* were not popular until Thomas D. Rice (1808–1860) borrowed Negro clothes and sang "Jim Crow." Surviving illustrations of Rice's routine capture the caricature: knees bent, hand raised, the other hand on hip, and the head positioned at a curiously comic angle. From this beginning evolved two main types of Negro impersonation that set the pattern for performers of "burnt-cork" specialties: the southern plantation hand, poor, crude, but happy-go-lucky (as personified in Jim Crow), and the ludicrous travesty of the white dandy. Comedy was essential to the success of the act, so most performers blended these animated Negro impersonations with improvised commentary on humorous subjects. At first, solo routines dominated Negro impersonation. **20**

Later, blackface specialists formed small bands of two or three singer-dancers and instrumentalists.

The Virginia Minstrels

The idea of a minstrel show originated in 1843 when Dan Emmett and the Virginia Minstrels opened a unique

Dan Emmett and the Virginia Minstrels originated the idea of a minstrel show. Theirs was an ensemble of four musicians who performed on banjo, violin, tambourine, and bones between sketches and comic banter. (Photo: Music Department, Sheet Music Collection, Free Library of Philadelphia)

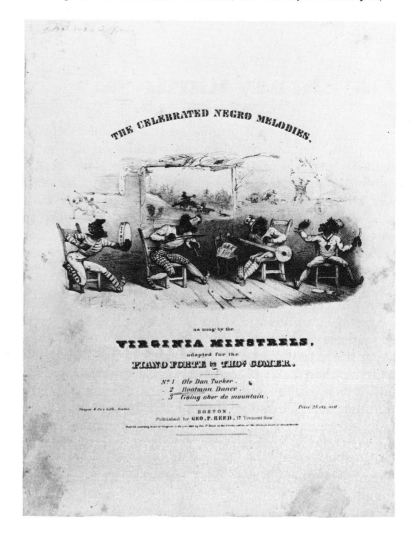

blackface act billed as a "novel, grotesque, original and surpassingly melodious Ethiopian Band" that introduced an historic new form to an evening's musical theater entertainment. Dressed in striped shirts, white trousers, and blue swallowtail calico coats, the ensemble of four musicians not only performed on banjo, violin, tambourine, and bones, but served as characters for continuous comic banter, sketches, and scenes. The Virginia Minstrels were less an act than a complete, self-sufficient show. With coordinated ensemble work supplemented by specific vocal, instrumental, and comedy assignments set within a two-act frame of variety acts and a sentimental Negro atmosphere, Dan Emmett and his Ethiopian Band set the format and style of early pre–Civil War minstrelsy.

The Christy Minstrels

The Virginia Minstrels originated the idea of a Minstrel Show, but the Christy Minstrels established its mature patterns and practices. Edwin Christy was the most famous and successful minstrel showman of his time. He sat his minstrels in a semicircle on the stage. He commissioned original songs for his shows, and he instituted the three-act minstrel show format. The first act presented variety entertainment. In this part, performers sat in a semicircle facing the audience while two "end-men," Mr. Tambo and Mr. Bones, engaged in gags and repartee with the centrally placed Mr. Interlocutor. Mr. Tambo played the tambourine and Mr. Bones played an instrument created out of the jawbone or rib bone of a horse, ox, or sheep that was struck, scraped, or rattled for sound. At prescribed intervals, individual performers would sing and dance, or the entire cast might perform a choral number. The act ended with a song by the entire company arranged in two choruses that concluded with a "walkaround" in which performers alternated in executing a brief specialty at the center of the company's semicircle. The second act, the "fantasia," presented cast members who performed their individual specialties. Par- **22**

The Christy Minstrels instituted the three-act minstrel show format that would later influence the development of vaudeville, revue, and burlesque. (Photo: Theatre Collection, Free Library of Philadelphia)

ticularly identified with this act were such routines as the playing of Paganini's *Variations on the Carnival of Venice* on a tin whistle, the extended sight gag of removing numerous layers of coats, shirts, and vests, and the "wench numbers" acted out by the female impersonators. The third act ended the show with a burlesque of some previous act, recent event, political oratory, or contemporary personality. The script of this burlesque was seldom more than a brief outline, but contemporary accounts attest to the skill of professional performers in improvising patter and action. These improvisations found their fullest expression in the burlesques of the most popular plays of the day. *Romeo and Juliet* became *Roman Nose and Suet*, while *Macbeth* was given as *Bad Breath, the Crane of Chowder*. Minstrel shows like these made the Christy Minstrels the premier organization during the heyday of minstrelsy, one that traveled as far as England where it captured the public's fancy and created the rage for minstrel entertainment.

Jokes, riddles, and puns generated the comedy. The "conundrums" that amused nineteenth-century audiences sounded like this:

Why is a man that's got the gout like a window?
Because he's full of *panes*.

Why do cats see in the dark?
'Cause they eat *light*.

Why is a dejected man like the root of a tongue?
'Cause he's down in the mouth.

Why is a quarrelsome man like a camel?
'Cause he's got his back up.

Why is a hog like a tree?
'Cause it *roots*.

Why is a dog like a tree?
'Cause it *barks*.

What kind of hair does a dog have?
Dog's hair.

Suppose an old woman tumbles overboard, what does she like?
Likes to be drowned.

Suppose a fly jumps into a milk-pan, what does he find?
A watery grave.

When is a young lady inclined for more beaux than one?
When she tries to *fascinate (fasten eight)*.

Why is the Union like a stone?
'Cause it's hard to *dissolve*.

Why is a portrait painter like a persimmon?
'Cause he draws your mouth.

What did Jonah get when the whale swallowed him?
He got sucked in.

When a dog scratches at the door for a bone, and gets no answer, what does he do?
Paws for a reply.

24

Why is a live dog's tail like the root of a tree?
'Cause it's farthest from the bark.

Why is the letter K like a pig's tail?
'Cause it's the end of por*k*.

Why is a quid of tobacco like a sneeze?
'Cause it's *a-chew*.

If some trees are known by their fruit, what ought a dog-wood tree to be known by?
Its bark.

The majority of minstrel troupes begged, borrowed, and stole these jokes in order to integrate them into the exchanges between Mr. Interlocutor and the end men:

INTERLOCUTOR: Gentlemen, be seated. *(Entire company sits down. Interlocutor walks over to first End-man, on right.)* Well, _____, I understand that you had a big party at your house last night.

END-MAN: Yes, my sister was celebrating.

INTERLOCUTOR: What was the celebration?

END-MAN: She was celebrating the tenth anniversary of her *thirtieth* birthday. *(Pause for laugh.)*

INTERLOCUTOR: I'm afraid your sister is entirely too loquacious.

END-MAN: And not only that, but she talks too much. *(Pause for laugh.)*

Or this:

INTERLOCUTOR: I saw you walking with a young lady yesterday.

END-MAN: Yes, and she saw you.

INTERLOCUTOR: I know she did—she smiled at me. What do you think of that? She was with him and she smiled at me.

END-MAN: Smiled at you? That's nothing. The first time I ever looked at you I thought I'd laugh my head off.

INTERLOCUTOR: Who is that young lady?

END-MAN: She's an oculist in Horn and Hardart's kitchen.

INTERLOCUTOR: An oculist?

END-MAN: Yes. She takes the eyes out of potatoes. She's related to the Burst family. Do you know John Burst?

INTERLOCUTOR: Very well indeed.

END-MAN: He's got three children.

INTERLOCUTOR: What are their names?

25

| END-MAN: | Alice May Burst, James Wood Burst, and Henry Will Burst. *(Laughs.)* They must be full of hot air and gas. |

Puns figured in most comic banter:

END-MAN:	What business are you in? I saw you with a lot of old tin cans going into a grocery store.
INTERLOCUTOR:	I'm in the canning business, canning pears, peaches, and tomatoes.
END-MAN:	Is that so? I'm in the wholesale dry goods business. So you're in the canning business, are you? What do you do with such a whole lot of pears and peaches?
INTERLOCUTOR:	Well, we eat what we *can*, and what we can't eat, we *can*.
END-MAN:	Eat what you can, and what you can't eat, you can! Just like my business.
INTERLOCUTOR:	How?
END-MAN:	We *sell* an order when we can *sell* it and when we can't *sell* it, why, we *can-cel* it. Eat what you can and what you can't eat, you can! You're a can can kind of a chump, you are.

Songs

Minstrel audiences came to hear the songs. You can't blame them, because the dramatic and theatrical elements of the minstrel show were subject to no standards beyond immediate popular appeal or individual performer preference. Consequently, many of the crude and predictable texts, the silly or nonsensical lyrics, and the tasteless low comedy sketches have passed into a much deserved oblivion. Not the tunes. Minstrelsy contributed the most popular and historically visible songs of the period, the best of which have survived to become the most beloved "folk" songs in the American repertory. These songs were simple: plain lyrics set to notes and harmonies drawn from an elementary musical vocabulary. That is not to say the songs were undistinguished. Simple and direct expression graces any art. So does an artistic attitude, the very beginning of which we can detect in some of the sentimental minstrel numbers. In order to capture **26** in song the substance and spirit of Negro plantation life, the best composers confined their material to the simple ideas and sounds of the narrow and rigidly prescribed world of the working slave. One such song that may have originated on a plantation but which was recorded by Dan Emmett around 1846 was the "Blue-tail Fly," known also as "Jimmy Crack Corn." As with most minstrel songs, the composer structured lyrics and melody to end in a lively refrain which contrasts markedly to the opening section.

> *When I was young I used to wait*
> *At master's side and hand his plate*
> *And pass the bottle when he got dry*
> *And brush away the blue-tail fly.*
> *Jimmy crack corn and I don't care*
> *Jimmy crack corn and I don't care*
> *Jimmy crack corn and I don't care*
> *Ol' master's gone a-way.*

If the music of the song is familiar to the reader, he or she should note the regular rhythm constantly maintained, the melodic motif formed by repeated notes, and the narrow compass of the total melodic profile. Such characteristics repeat in many of the banjo tunes of minstrelsy, particularly in "Polly Wolly Doodle" and "Buffalo Gals." The latter song enjoyed enormous popularity with audiences throughout the country, less for the composer's innovative use of syncopated rhythm than for a practice peculiar to minstrel showmanship which altered the title of songs to flatter the town booked for a performance. Thus, "Buffalo Gals" became "Charleston Gals" or "Louisville Gals." Sentimental songs that celebrated scenes from domestic life were particular audience favorites. Thatcher, Primrose, and West's Minstrels popularized this lullaby in the late 1880s:

> *Baby is sleeping so cosy and fair,*
> *While mother sits near in her old oaken chair,*
> *Her foot on the rocker the cradle she swings,*
> *And though baby slumbers, he hears what she sings.*
> CHORUS
> *Rock-a-bye baby on the tree top,*
> *When the wind blows the cradle will rock,*
> *When the bough breaks the cradle will fall,*

And down will come baby, cradle and all.
Oh, rock-a-bye, rock-a-bye, mother is near,
Then rock-a-bye, rock-a-bye, nothing to fear,
For angels of slumber are hovering near,
So rock-a-bye baby, mother is here.
Grandma sits knitting close by the fireplace,
With snowy white hair and a smile on her face,
The years have passed by, yet it does not seem long,
Since she rocked baby's papa to sleep with that song.

CHORUS

Dear little baby their joy and their pride,
Long may he be with them whatever betide,
The kitchen, the cradle, that tender refrain,
In mem'ry will linger that lul-la-by strain.

CHORUS

The more prosperous troupes commissioned special material for their shows, much like this "New Ethiopian Medley" of twenty-three airs arranged by H. Angelo expressly for E. F. Dixey.

1. FOLKS THAT PUT ON AIRS

   Oh! white folks, listen will you now,
   Dis darkie's gwine to sing;
   I've hit upon a subject now,
   I think will be · · ·

2. BEHIND DE OLD GUM TREE

   Behind de old gum tree
   A coon declined one day,
   A blackbird dar he see · · ·

3. OLD FOLKS AT HOME

   'Way down upon de Swanee river,
   Far, far away,
   Dar's whar · · ·

4. O, SUSANNA

   I had a dream de other night,
   When everything was still,
   I thought I saw Susanna · · ·

5. SITTIN' ON A RAIL

   Sittin' on a rail, sittin' on a rail,
   Sittin' on a rail, sittin' on a rail,
   With · · ·

6. DANDY JIM

   Dandy Jim ob Caroline;
   My old massa told me, oh,
   I was de best-looking nigger in de county, oh
   I looked in de glass and found · · ·

7. ZIP COON

   A possum on a log, a playing with his toes,
   A possum on a log, a playing · · ·

8. DIXIE LAND

I wish I was in Dixie: oh, oh, oh, oh;
In Dixie Land I'll take · · ·

9. OLD AUNT SALLY

My old Aunt Sally;
Ra, re, ri, ro, round de corner · · ·

10. BOWLING GREEN

Once upon a time, once upon a time,
  Dis old darkey used to go
To hear · · ·

11. CAMPTOWN RACES

De Camptown ladies sing dis song;
  Du-da, du-da;
Camptown race-track five mile long;
  Du-da, du-da, day.
I went down dar with · · ·

12. LUCY NEAL

My poor Lucy Neal,
My poor Lucy Neal,
If I had her · · ·

13. WALK IN DE PARLOR

'Way down South, close by de moon,
I learnt to sing dis lovely tune;
Niggers dar dey grow so fat,
On dar chins dey · · ·

14. JIM CROW

Turn about and wheel about,
  And do just so;
Every time I wheel about,
  I jump · · ·

15. GOING OVER THE MOUNTAIN

'Way down in Kentucky brake,
  Rum tum, diddle um a da,
A darkey lived, dey call him · · ·

16. THE FINE OLD GENTLEMAN

A fine old colored gemman,
One ob de tallest · · ·

17. ROSA LEE

When I lived in Tennessee,
  u-li, a-li, o-li, e,
I went courting · · ·

18. BEWITCHING DINAH CROW

Bewitching Dinah Crow,
Bewitching Dinah Crow,
  Who was drowned and den found dead · · ·

19. NELLY WAS A LADY

Down on de Mississippi floating,
Long time I travelled · · ·

20. NANCY TILL

Down in the cane-brake, close by de mill,
Libs a yaller gal, and dey call her Nancy Till;
She knowed dat I love her, she knowed it long;
I'se gwine to serenade her and sing · · ·

21. I'M OFF TO BALTIMORE

Come love, come, you need not fear,
My boat lies over · · ·

22. CRACO-VIENNA

In South Carolina, whar I was born,
I chop de wood and husk de corn;
A roasted ear to de house I bring,
De driver kotch me and I sing · · ·

23. GOOD-BYE, WHITE FOLKS

Good-bye, white folks all, I'se gwine away
*   to leave you;*
Good-bye, white folks all, don't let my
*   parting grieve you.*

Although the songs of minstrelsy maintained their popularity well into the twentieth century, even the most distinguished of them lack the thematic and structural development needed for a mature theater song. Even today, the listener cannot escape the impression that these songs are over too soon. Any song that depends solely on repetition to flesh out performance commands little potential for expressive depth, dramatic scope, or theatrical function.

Dances

One thing a minstrel song could do was provide lively accompaniment for dance. Unlike the improvised dances of the slaves, the minstrel dances were fashioned for the professional stage to which they added the flavor, styles, and motifs of the plantation, country life, and the frontier. As in today's musicals, the dancing appeared to be spontaneous, but the animated characterization along with the variety of movement patterns were all worked out to exploit the showmanship of the performers and encourage audience reaction to it. Minstrel dancing avoided the polite and restrained steps of social dances in favor of   **30** the free and open movements of a liberated face and body. Although individual performers made widespread use of dance in their songs and "specialties," minstrel dance achieved fullest expression in the *cakewalk* and the *walkaround*. Minstrelsy popularized the cakewalk, a dance that was adapted to the stage from a custom of American Negros on southern plantations before the Civil War. Originally, the cakewalk was a contest in which dancing couples executed walking steps and figures in precise formations as if in mimicry of the white man's attitudes and manners. Since the couples were eliminated by consensus until the best couple remained to accept a festively adorned cake, the dance originated the expression "to take the cake" and came to be known as the cakewalk. The dance adapted well to the stage, where its most salient feature was a promenade executed in a high-leg prance with a backward tilt of head, shoulders, and upper torso. The walkaround began as a solo dance but evolved into an ensemble song-and-dance number that concluded the first act of the minstrel show. In the opening part of the dance, the comedians would step forth and sing a stanza, then the entire company would sing or dance as they walked around the stage. A walkaround may be regarded as a crude nineteenth-century equivalent of the production number with all the performance artillery on stage lighting up the sky with bursts of solo and ensemble images that explode in company song and dance. The walkaround was as eagerly anticipated then as the big musical numbers are today. In fact, Dan Emmett's main job with the Bryant's Minstrels late in his career was to write the words and the music for the all-important walkaround. His most famous effort? "Dixie"!

Dan Emmett

Of the creative artists generated by professional blackface entertainments, Dan Emmett was the earliest to create and perform important original material. An early interest in Negro songs led him to master the banjo and to write for that instrument some of the most popular songs of minstrelsy's early period: "De Boatman's Dance," "Old Dan Tucker," and "Dixie." Although he performed to great acclaim as a singer, comedian, and instrumentalist, his writing of comedy sketches, speeches, plays, music, and lyrics put him right in the center of the "Ethiopian business." Although his work was the unpolished expression of a rather narrow aesthetic vision, its sentimentality guaranteed success, catering as it did to mid-century northern audiences concerned with the moral and political evils of slavery. Emmett said what the audience wanted to hear, as his music approximated the sound of Negro spirituals in its not coincidental use of the minor-third interval. The sound was so right for the times that one of the composer's songs became the most beloved or hated hymns of the Civil War. "Dixie" became the smash hit song of New York when introduced as a walk-around by the Bryant's Minstrels. Because of lax copyright enforcement procedures, minstrel companies throughout the United States appropriated the song as their own and spread its fame everywhere. In the South, new lyrics were added and the song was adopted as the favorite battle hymn of the Confederate armies.

Stephen Foster

The most famous American composer to introduce original songs to the public in minstrel shows was Stephen Foster (1826–1864). When we listen to "Old Folks at Home" ("Way down upon the Swanee River"), "Camptown Races," "O Susanna," or "My Old Kentucky Home," images come to mind of plantations in the Deep South, summer evenings, melancholy songs with banjo accompaniment. We picture Mr. Foster resplendent in an immaculate white suit rocking on a veranda framed by the Corinthian columns of an antebellum mansion. What a lovely cinematic image. What fiction! Stephen Foster lived, worked, and died in the North, particularly in the

Edwin Christy commissioned new "Ethiopian" songs for his minstrel shows. (Photo: Music Department, Sheet Music Collection, Free Library of Philadelphia)

area around Pittsburgh, where "O Susanna" premiered at the Eagle Ice Cream Saloon. It was minstrelsy that originated and sustained the composer's identification with the South, just as it did with Emmett and scores of northern artists whose profession traded in theatrical illusions of romanticized plantation life. Foster turned to minstrelsy only to further his career as a genteel songwriter. Minstrelsy turned to Foster for fresh material like "Camptown Races" and "Old Folks at Home." Such a marriage of convenience and profit drew the composer to Edwin Christy of the Christy Minstrels who responded to Foster's determination to become the best "Ethiopian" songwriter by featuring these plantation melodies in his celebrated shows. Stephen Foster was not a trained musician, yet he wrote over two hundred songs. From a musical technique burdened by repetitious ideas, elementary harmonies, and predictable rhythms issued songs like "O Susanna," a brief and direct novelty number that pretends to little and holds no surprises. Yet the song became an overwhelming minstrel favorite and the recognized theme song of the pioneers during the California Gold Rush. Why? Simple melodies that conform to popular taste succeed, and Foster's melodies met both conditions. That Foster's music also engaged interest, lifted the spirit, and provoked deeply felt emotion only immortalized his contribution.

James Bland

After the Civil War, emancipated Negroes with musical or dramatic talent turned to minstrelsy as the most appropriate avenue to a new life in the mainstream of American show business. When the all-Negro troupes entered the field, they adapted its conventions, even the burnt cork makeup and the thickened lips. The most successful troupes introduced to a diminishing public some of the most celebrated Negro writers and entertainers of the day. Of these, none was more important than James A. Bland. Like Dan Emmett and Stephen Foster, James Bland was born and bred in the North, the well-educated son of a man who was among the first Negroes in the United States to receive a college education. He entered minstrelsy as an entertainer, but went on to contribute to the sentimental plantation song repertory the words and music to "Carry Me Back to Old Virginny" and "In the Evening by the Moonlight." He wrote walkarounds, too, like "O, Dem Golden Slippers," a great favorite in the United States and England. Unfortunately, comparatively little is known of Bland's creative output. He was a natural musician capable of brilliant instrumental im- **34**

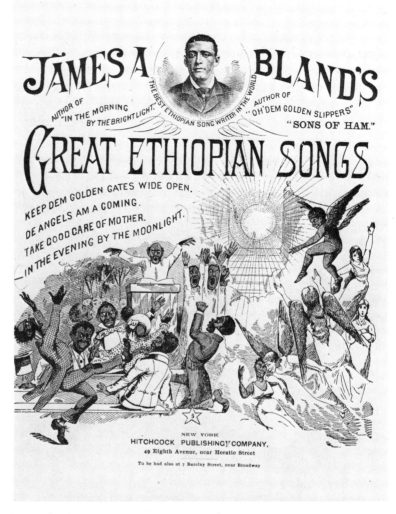

James Bland entered minstrelsy as an entertainer but went on to become the most celebrated Negro writer of plantation melodies. (Photo: Music Department, Sheet Music Collection, Free Library of Philadelphia)

provisations. Since he sang and accompanied himself, there was no need in his lifetime to write down his material. Although the Library of Congress retains just thirty-eight copies of his songs, tradition credits him with over six hundred works. If only for those songs that remain, Bland must be considered a worthy successor in the artistic tradition of his predecessors, the last bright light in the sunset years of American minstrelsy.

Decline

Although the minstrel form continued well into the twentieth century, it lost creative energy by the 1870s and declined rapidly in cultural prominence. Where early and mature minstrel shows traded on a few versatile performers equipped with little or no scenery, the later companies mounted spectacles of fifty, sixty, and even one hundred entertainers, all equipped with elaborate and expensive surroundings. The shift in focus from true minstrelsy to spectacle encountered criticism from concerned advocates. On July 12, 1893, an article entitled "Old Time Minstrelsy" appeared with the following argument:

Minstrelsy declined when large troupes attempted to win back the old audience with elaborate shows. (Photo: Byron, The Byron Collection, Museum of the City of New York)

However numerous the company, however extensive the programme, however expensive the talent, however elaborate the costumes, however gorgeous the mountings, there is still something lacking in the minstrel shows; what is lacking are the half-dozen versatile entertainers with blackened faces, sharp wits and limber legs.

Those entertainers would never return, at least to the minstrel show. A public faced with the harsh realities of the Reconstruction period became disaffected with the stereotyped, romanticized illusions of southern plantation life. Poised on the brink of the Gilded Age, affluent audiences demanded spectacular entertainments to which the format of minstrelsy did not respond effectively. When public tastes change, so must the popular theater. But rather than abandon the minstrel show entirely, the gods of the theater chose to reincarnate its acts into later, even more popular musical theater forms. The variety acts segment grew into vaudeville, the "specialties" act led to the revue, and the burlesque finale pointed the way for the burlesque of Weber and Fields. What was best remained. What could be transformed was. What was weak and unsound disappeared. Fate had the tradition of American musical theater well in hand.

3

VAUDEVILLE

When the Albee Theatre in Brooklyn opened on January 19, 1925, the newspapers described the palace designed to accommodate the best in vaudeville and first-run silent movies as "the most beautiful theater in the world." As audiences gaped at the grand hall with Italian marble stairways, the 40-by-70-foot silver, gray, gold, and black Czechoslovakian rug made on the largest loom in the world, the valuable paintings, and the three spectacular crystal chandeliers, hardy vaudevillians accustomed to more spartan surroundings cautiously oriented themselves to a backstage environment complete with laundry, several kitchenettes, twenty dressing rooms (each with private bath), and a nursery for the children. On opening day, Al Jolson sat in the audience. So did Eddie Cantor. On stage were Bill "Bojangles" Robinson, the comedy team of Smith and Dale, and a bill of other big-time performers. Motion pictures had arrived, but vaudeville was big business still, "the greatest amusement buy in the world."

In those days, vaudeville had been around for fifty years, entertaining American audiences with a show form consisting of unrelated acts following one another in succession. Although the vaudeville concept may have originated in fifteenth-century France where the villagers of Val de Vire entertained themselves with ballads and satirical songs, the American stage form began in 1865 when a former minstrel showman named Tony Pastor opened a theater for variety entertainment in Paterson, New Jersey. Since variety acts were standard fare in the first act

Tony Pastor popularized variety entertainment, shows consisting of unrelated acts following one another in succession. (Photo: Theatre Collection, Free Library of Philadelphia)

of the minstrel show, Pastor's enterprise rested less on theatrical innovation than on an audacious social policy that eliminated the drinking bar from the theater, removed all objectionable or suggestive elements from performance material, and directed the entire commercial operations to appeal to women and children. What foresight! Tony Pastor gambled on the idea of family fare as big business—and won. He publicized and enforced **40**

THE EMPIRE PROGRAMME

Coming !

Week Commencing Monday Matinee,
October 22.

Matinee Every Day, 15c. and 25c.

Willard Simms & Co.
Presenting "FLINDER'S FURNISHED FLAT."

Cliff Gordon
The German Politician.

Selbini & Grovini
Juggling, Tumbling and Acrobatic Bicycling

Torbay
Comedy Silhouettist.

Girl Behind the Drum

Jno. and Bertha Rich
The Jolly Duo.

Special Added Attraction

Spessardy's Bears
Direct from the New York Hippodrome.

Vaudeville prospered for over fifty years by directing its entire commercial operation to women and children. (Photo: Theatre Collection, Free Library of Philadelphia)

a policy of no smoking, no drinking, and no vulgarity while he booked acts like Harrigan and Hart in "After the War," Gus Williams in his original Dutch character songs and sayings, and Madam Zittella and the Varella Brothers. At Tony Pastor's Theatre in New York, the program announced:

Extra! Extra! Extra!
60 Hams Given away Monday Evening
10 Barrels of Flour given away Wednesday
10 Tons of Coal Given away Saturday Evening
80 Prizes

When Tony Pastor's career as a big-time impresario faded, E. F. Albee led the crusade for scrupulous purity in vaudeville entertainment. Albee was a strict and stern

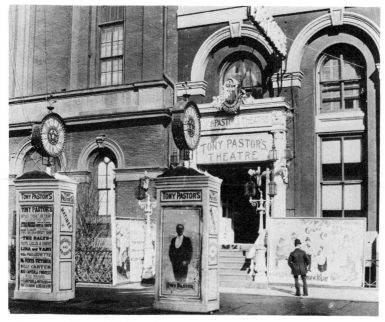

Tony Pastor's Theatre in New York, the citadel of early vaudeville. (Photo: Byron, the Byron Collection, Museum of the City of New York)

censor who set the moral tone for the Palace and the entire Keith circuit with notices like the following:

> Remember, this theater caters to ladies and gentlemen and children. Vulgarity will not be tolerated. Check with the manager if you have any doubt about it. Don't use the words hell, damn, devil, cockroach, spit, etc. . . .

Any act was ordered to cut objectionable material. If the order was ignored, the act was cut. Although many vaudevillians referred to the Keith operation as the "Sunday School circuit," it was censorship like this that made vaudeville unique and kept its box office phenomenally successful for fifty years. In the early decades of the twentieth century, vaudeville was so deeply established an institution of respectable amusement that Sarah Bernhardt shared bills with dog acts, wire walkers, midgets, and contortionists. Show business entered a golden age of new and gaudy showplaces, dazzling showmen, and nearly two thousand theaters featuring weekly programs of nine acts to the bill. So deep was America in "two-a-day" circuits and chains that an actor, not recognizing **42** his booking, felt obliged to ask his agent, "What is it? Smalltime, medium smalltime, big smalltime, little big time, medium big time, or big time?"

Acts

Variety acts sustained vaudeville. Singers, dancers, actors, and comics shared billing with the specialty acts of magicians, midgets, monkeys, dogs, and elephants. Many a bill featured a "dumb act," a dance or animal act which required no speaking or a European troupe of acrobats unable to speak the English language. Kiddy acts drew a favorable audience. *Variety* identified sixty-two "school acts" playing the big-time circuit in 1913. Comics prospered, and some of the funniest routines were musical. When "musicians" played out of tune, on their heads or with strange unmusical instruments, America laughed. As Charles and Louise Samuels wrote in *Once Upon a Stage,* *

> Vaudeville drew on all of the other performing arts and presented opera singers, ballet dancers, circus stars, sports champions, minstrels, serious musicians, . . . Swiss bell ringers, . . . midgets from Germany, tumblers from Japan, tabloid Wild West Shows, . . . horses that could count, female impersonators, trained seals, skating bears, monologists, harmonica players, xylophonists, fire-eaters, unicyclists, and everything else that was new, startling, . . . sensational or unbelievable.

Each act was placed on a bill in a sequence determined by rank or type of act. An early vaudeville bill looked like the one on page 44.

By 1924, big-time management demanded more sophistication in acts, performers, and programming. A streamlined quality program for the B. F. Keith's Riverside Theatre is shown on page 45.

The vaudeville bill appeared to be a spontaneous

* From *Once Upon a Stage* by Charles and Louise Samuels. New York: Dodd, Mead, and Co., 1974. Reprinted with permission of the publisher and the Sterling Lord Agency, Inc. Copyright © 1974 by Charles and Louise Samuels.

43

Programme

The New Grand Refined Vaudeville
Washington City
Season—Eighteen ninety-nine - nineteen hundred

Burke and Chase—Managers

Evening prices . . . Box seats $1.00, Orchestra $.50, Balcony .25
Daily Matinees . . . Box seats $1.00, Entire House .25

Note: The acts are not always placed in the order
of their appearance. See cards displayed
at the sides of the stage.

Overture—Capt. Harrington's March—C.W. Bennet
Ackley's Orchestra
Wormwood's Dog and Monkey Circus—"The Largest, Most Novel
and Most Famous, 'Animal Act' Now Before the Public."
Arthur Rigby—Monologist
Will Matthews & Harris—Nellie
"Adam the Second"

Intermission—10 minutes

Overture—The Butterfly—Theo. Bendix
Solo for Flute and Clarinet
Ackley's Orchestra
Charles M.—Seay & Hendrie—Anita
In Mr. Seay's Satirical Comedy "Dollars & Dogs"
Mr. & Mrs. Jimmie Barry—In a Comedy Sketch,
entitled, "Mrs. Wilkin's Boy"
Carl Dammann Troupe—Great European Acrobatic Act
The American Biograph—owned and operated by
the American Metroscope Company, N.Y.
Invention of Herman Casler. A.L. Steele, Operator.
Scenes.   Canoeing on the Charles River. Trained
Elephant and Trick Ponies. Artificial
Hatching of Chickens. Buffalo Fire
Department Responding to an Alarm.
Policeman, Servant and Tramp in Kitchen.
Launching of Battleship Vengeance. Young
Man and Sweetheart on an Outing. On the
Canadian Pacific Railway. Fishing Johnny
from a well. Astor Battery, 33rd U.S.
Infantry in Honolulu. Angry Husband.

sequence of assorted attractions, but skilled managers put
together each program from a standard plan for the house
or the circuit. The popular acts competed not only for
big-time bookings, but for the most desirable spot on the   **44**

```
                          Overture

My Best Girl                                    Walter Donaldson

                    Riverside Theatre Orchestra

Durkin's European Novelty—A pantomime Dog and Monkey
                          offering.
Spadaro—Italy's leading comedian
Valerie Bergere and her Company
Iren Ricardo
Dora & Ed Ford Revue "Premiere Dancers"
Douglas Leavitt & Ruth Mary Lockwood
                        Miss Nora Bayes
"Our Own Nora"        "The Famous International Singer of Songs."
Chevalier Brothers "Entertaining Entertainers"
                        Exit March
```

bill. Acts avoided the "bottom-liner" spot, a fate known to the professionals as "dog billing," so far down on the poster advertisements that only dogs could be expected to identify the act. The stars on the circuit expected the most prestigious spot on the bill, the spot just before intermission or just before closing. Imagine the competitive climate in a business where management booked only nine acts out of the estimated twenty thousand available. George A. Gottlieb booked for the Palace Theatre in New York during the golden days of vaudeville. He explained how top management laid out the standard nine-act bill:

We usually select a "dumb act" for the first act on the bill. It may be a dancing act, some good animal act, or any act that makes a good impression and will not be spoiled by the late arrivals seeking their seats. Therefore, it sometimes happens that we make use of a song-and-dance turn, or any other little act that does not depend on its words being heard.

For number two position we select an interesting act of the sort recognized as a typical "vaudeville act." It may be almost anything at all, though it should be more entertaining than the first act. For this reason it often happens that a good man-and-woman singing act is placed here. This position on the bill is to "settle" the audience and to prepare it for the show.

With number three position we count on waking up the audience. The show has been properly started and from now on it must build right up to the finish. So we offer a comedy-dramatic sketch—a playlet that wakens the interest and holds the audience every minute with a culminative effect that comes to its laughter-climax at the "curtain," or any other kind of act that

The Palace Theatre, New York. 1928. Pinnacle
of big-time entertainment during the golden days
of vaudeville. (Photo: Theatre and Music Collection, Museum of the City of New York)

is not of the same order as the preceding turn, so that, having
laid the foundations, we may have the audience wondering what
is to come next.

For number four position we must have a "corker" of an act—
and a "name." It must be the sort of act that will rouse the
audience to expect still better things, based on the fine performance of the past numbers. Maybe this act is the first big punch
of the show; anyway it must strike home and build up the interest
for the act that follows.

And here for number five position, a big act, and at the same
time another big name, must be presented. Or it might be a
big dancing act—one of those delightful novelties vaudeville
likes so well. In any event this act must be as big a "hit" as
any on the bill. It is next to intermission and the audience must
have something really worth while to talk over. And so we select
one of the best acts on the bill to crown the first half of the
show. **46**

The first act after intermission, number six on the bill, is a difficult position to fill, because the act must not let down the carefully built-up tension of interest and yet it must not be stronger than the acts that are to follow. Very likely there is chosen a strong vaudeville specialty, with comedy well to the fore. Perhaps a famous comedy dumb act is selected, with the intention of getting the audience back in its seats without too many conspicuous interruptions of what is going on on the stage. Any sort of act that makes a splendid start-off is chosen, for there has been a fine first half and the second half must be built up again—of course the process is infinitely swifter in the second half of the show—and the audience brought once more into a delighted-expectant attitude.

Therefore, the second act after intermission—number seven—must be stronger than the first. It is usually a full stage act and again must be another big name. Very likely it is a big playlet, if another sketch has not been presented earlier on the bill. It may be a comedy playlet or even a serious dramatic playlet, if the star is a fine actor or actress and the name is well known. Or it may be anything at all that builds up the interest and appreciation of the audience to welcome the "big" act that follows.

For here in number eight position—next to closing, in a nine-act bill—the comedy hit of the show is usually placed. It is one of the acts for which the audience has been waiting. Usually it is one of the famous "single" man or "single" woman acts that vaudeville has made such favorites.

And now we have come to the act that closes the show. We count on the fact that some of the audience will be going out. Many have only waited to see the chief attraction of the evening, before hurrying off to their after-theatre supper and dance. So we spring a big "flash." It must be an act that does not depend for its success upon being heard perfectly. Therefore a "sight" act is chosen, an animal act maybe, to please the children, or a Japanese troupe with their gorgeous kimonos and vividly harmonizing stage draperies, or a troupe of white-clad trapeze artists flying against a background of black. What ever the act is, it must be a showy act, for it closes the performance and sends the audience home pleased with the program to the very last minute.

Artists

All vaudeville performers were called "artists," and among the twenty-five thousand artists who played in four thousand theaters from 1878 to 1925 were the outstanding show business personalities of the day. Lillian

Russell made her debut at Tony Pastor's Bowery Theatre

Lillian Russell—"The American Beauty." Her pleasant singing voice and imposing physical presence sustained a career that eventually made her the best-known woman in America. (Photo: Theatre Collection, Free Library of Philadelphia)

and went on to become the era's most celebrated beauty. George M. Cohan broke into the business with his family in an act billed as the Four Cohans. Houdini captured more publicity for his escape stunts at the height of his career than any single celebrity. It made him the number-one draw in vaudeville. Among the comics, Jack Murphy rocked the galleries with monologues and jokes like, "I had a nightmare in bed, but the bed was a little buggy—so I hitched the mare to the buggy and drove out of town." W. C. Fields did his "pool table" scene, and Weber and Fields did their "Dutch act." Vaudeville gave women equal opportunity to rise to stardom. Audiences loved Nora Bayes and never tired of her cool and effortless "Shine on, Harvest Moon." Opera singers represented **48**

Harry Houdini—escape artist, magician, master of the "challenge act," and one of the greatest showmen of vaudeville. (Photo: Theatre and Music Collection, Museum of the City of New York)

the classiest group of headliners, and many established divas took "a turn" on the stage, as did the top legitimate actresses who appeared in cuttings, one-acts, or entire scenes. Alla Nazimova played *War Brides* throughout the years of World War I. Sarah Bernhardt reduced her public to a "sodden mass" with the last act of *The Lady of the Camellias.* Less sedate women rose to the top another way. Eva Tanguay, the "I Don't Care Girl," skirted decency and the wrath of censors with "It's All Been Done Before, But Not the Way I Do It." Mae West sang songs like "If You Don't Like My Peaches Why Do You Shake My Tree?" The list goes on: Will Rogers, Irene and Vernon Castle, Ethel Barrymore, Fanny Brice, George Jessel, and Sophie Tucker. Vaudeville attracted the best for "the **49** best entertainment money could buy."

Poise, skill, and an unrivaled talent for dramatizing a song gave Miss Nora Bayes, "The Famous International Singer of Songs" one of the great solo female acts of vaudeville. (Photo: Theatre and Music Collection, Museum of the City of New York)

Songs

The vaudeville stage became the public forum for the most popular songs in America. Seasoned performers who vied with each other for audience acceptance knew that fresh, popular, and suitable material went far to distinguish them from all other acts of their type. Consequently, ambitious artists wrote, commissioned, or stole songs for their act. The songs were an odd and varied lot. Bright and easy tunes in 3/4 time set the tone of most song and dance routines. When a vaudeville baritone named Charles Lawlor wrote "Sidewalk of New 50

The "Divine" Sarah Bernhardt. Her physical beauty, magnificent speaking voice, highly theatrical acting style and personal notoriety insured spectacularly successful vaudeville engagements. (Photo: Theatre and Music Collection, Museum of the City of New York)

York" (1894), the response was so overwhelming that the song became the unofficial anthem of the city of New York. Few songs are more typical of the period and its entertainments.

REFRAIN

East side,
West side,
All around the town.
The tots sang "ring'a'rosie"
London Bridge is falling down.
Boys and girls together
Me and Mamie O'Rorke
Tripped the light fantastic
On the sidewalks of New York.

Easy songs of lilting melody persisted throughout the early days of vaudeville. Like "In the Good Old Summertime" and "Waltz Me Around Again, Willie," they lingered long enough to become standard fare for many blazer-and-cane soft-shoe acts. Only the sentimental ballad flourished as its tender, soulful alternative. Family audiences rushed to heave and sigh at sirupy songs that glorified home, morality, friendship, virtue, devotion, and mother. None was more successful than "After the Ball," a sad and woeful tale of mistaken identity that went on from a premier in a Milwaukee vaudeville theater to become the first popular song to sell several million copies of sheet music. The song couldn't miss—and didn't. It reflected the standards and morals of its time, appealed to the formidable family sheet music market, and gave the crafty performer the opportunity to squeeze every ounce of emotion out of a willingly susceptible audience. Other sentimental ballads survived, like "When You Were Sixteen" and "Sweet Adeline"; the more effusive examples—like "Gold Will Buy Most Anything But a True Girl's Heart" or "The Lost Little Child"—did not. Vaudeville originated and popularized the specialty songs that sustained the character or ethnic acts. Irish characters singing "My Wild Irish Rose" or "Sweet Rosie O'Grady" thrived in a time of widespread European immigration. The comedians turned to songs like "I Wish I Were Single Again," while black and blackface vaudevillians utilized the robust and rhythmic "coon songs."

The popular song in America developed in form and content during the fifty years of vaudeville's ascendency. The early songs resorted invariably to sad stories told in an intolerably long verse that set up a sentimental refrain. "After the Ball" requires three repetitions of a sixty-four-measure verse each followed by a thirty-two-measure refrain to complete the song. The refrain commands the dominant musical interest. The plotted verse commands the dominant lyric interest. The problem is this: The song cannot match word strength to music strength. In the verse, a strong story fights weak music; in the refrain, strong music fights a weaker idea. Another problem typical of the period: the musical construction of the refrain seldom varied from AA or AB form. (See **52**

Vaudeville built more showplaces across the United States than any other form of entertainment. In New York, only Hammerstein's Victoria Theatre rivaled the Palace for big-time attractions. (Photo: Byron, The Byron Collection, Museum of the City of New York)

benefit of script, director, choreographer, or dramatic context. Each artist learned from experience how to capture an audience, pace a performance, and respond to a crisis. Vaudeville bred discipline into its artists. Flexibility, too. If management gave an act five minutes, the act played five minutes. If management gave an act ten, it played ten. Vaudeville built more showplaces across the United States than any other form of entertainment. It gave the American musical theater at least two thousand new places to be, to experiment, to grow and be acclaimed. For fifty years, vaudeville rode American optimism to fame and fortune, and many expected the combination to go on forever. A contemporary critic of vaudeville wrote:

I am no prophet, but one thing seems certain, and that is that vaudeville will always be with us if for no other reason than its cheapness. In these difficult times there are few people who care to pay two dollars for an orchestra seat at a musical show. Bellamy, in *Looking Backward*, predicts that the time will come when by merely turning a handle we will be able to bring music, lectures and other entertainments into our homes. But that is just a pleasing and improbable fantasy of an imaginative author. In this world of reality if we want convenient, inexpensive entertainment, we have to go out and get it, and it is impossible to imagine anything that can be a substitute for vaudeville.

Now, vaudeville theaters fall to make way for office buildings and parking lots. In Brooklyn, the "most beautiful theater in the world" has given way to a shopping mall. The brass ticket booth and a cue box to announce performers were saved for the mall and the Brooklyn Museum, but somewhere in a recent landfill is buried the remains of the great Italian marble stairways.

4

BURLESQUE

A courtroom scene. The actors look frayed and curiously off-balance. The trial begins. Nonsense everywhere. Suddenly, the judge begins to shoot peas through a straw at the jury. Confusion. The judge reacts extravagantly. "Order in the court!" "Order in the court!" Is there order? No. The judge has hit himself on the head with the gavel. He recovers. The trial resumes. A witness. Female. Voluptuous. A carefully contrived situation unfolds. Dialogue litters the stage with double entendres. Suddenly, an unexpected turn. Roughhouse. Slapstick. Finally, pandemonium. The scene ends. The audience roars.

That was burlesque.

According to the old-timers, it was the only true burlesque, namely, low-comedy parody complemented by the exhibition of girls in tights who displayed ample proportions of the nineteenth century female anatomy never before seen in public. Oh, the shame of Lydia Thompson and her English Blondes, corruptors of the men of 1869 with their "wanton thighs and legs," or Adah Isaacs Menken, costumed in a flesh-colored, form-clinging body stocking dashing across a stage strapped to a horse, or the final indignity of vigorous comedy being made to give way to "hootchie-kootchie" acts, oriental dancers, "Salome" dancers, interpretive dancers, control artists, shimmy shakers, tassel dancers, exotics, and strippers. Like the Roman god Janus who came into the world having two faces each symbolizing his powers, so did burlesque emerge with two faces, one turned toward low comedy, the other toward female anatomy. When the 58

Maggie Arlington. The old burlesque featured the exhibition of girls in tights who displayed the ample proportions of the nineteenth-century female anatomy never before seen in public. (Photo: Theatre and Music Collection, Museum of the City of New York)

latter prevailed, burlesque squandered its powers and degenerated into dirt and squalor like no other American musical theater form. We must follow that rise and fall. There are lessons to be learned.

Origins

American burlesque evolved from the one-act parody English burlesque where dialogue in rhymed couplets pursued humor through a relentless sequence of puns. Wisely, American producers mounted less aristocratic productions for local audiences by eliminating the cou-

Credit the enormous popularity of Lydia Thompson and her English Blondes to beefy girls displayed in living tableaux, the can can costumed with ruffled drawers, and ribald songs spiced with double entendres. (Photo: Theatre and Music Collection, Museum of the City of New York)

plets and retaining the satire. Gradually, the burlesques threw off the foreign mantle of restraint and decorum in favor of a more casual, comfortable, and well-fitting attire. Improvisation was much favored in the new style, more so than loyalty to character, plot, dialogue, or form. Add to this a growing vogue for the spectacular and the extravagant in entertainment and a unique form emerged. Although nineteenth century management employed the names *burlesque, spectacle, and extravaganza* to publicize their productions, the term *burlesque* generally referred to a musical sex-and-comedy-travesty entertainment, while the spectacle and the extravaganza by-

60

passed satiric content for awesome visual effects. The use of all three names in a descriptive title was not uncommon. The *Boston Ray* of May 13, 1878, proclaimed that the Calville Folly Company production of *Babes in the Wood* was a "New, Grand and Glittering Pantomimic Burlesque Extravaganza." A Boston playbill, the *Player*, heralded *White Faun* as a "New Fairy Burlesque Spectacular Extravaganza." Whatever the name, the musical theater tradition inherited another indigenous popular form: spectacular musical entertainments with girls and gags, satire and slang.

Specific "for men only" productions began around 1868. Michael Bennett Leavitt, the "Father of Burlesque," enticed the worldly into the theater with an

Management advertised *The White Faun* as a "New Fairy Burlesque, Spectacular Extravaganza." (Photo: J. Clarence Davies Collection, Museum of the City of New York)

MARCHE D'AIKA AMAZONIAN.

AS PERFORMED IN THE "WHITE FAWN", AT NIBLOS, N.Y.
NEWYORK,
Published by DODWORTH & SON, 6 Astor Place.

amusement that opened with the "spiel" of the "candy butcher" who paraded up and down the aisles of the theater pandering cheap boxes of candy reputed to contain valuable prizes or forbidden booklets devoted to "woman's hidden charms." The show itself followed the general three-act pattern of minstrelsy, but with one major innovation: a finale called the "Extra Added Attraction." Here, the more disreputable shows featured the "hootchie-kootchie" dance. Conservative managers dared nothing more than to schedule athletic contests like manly exhibitions of the art of self-defense.

An authentic burlesque show of the period offered a program like the one on pages 63–64.

The old burlesque was popular and profitable theater. In the boom years before World War I, stock companies operated out of large cities. Runs were long and steady, and a full season implied continuous performance from late August through late May. The major burlesque companies toured the United States on two distinct and highly competitive circuits known as the eastern wheel and the western wheel. The *wheel* in burlesque corresponded to the *circuit* in Vaudeville—a standardized system to control the mechanics and business operation of touring entertainments. The shows on a wheel contracted for a given number of performances on a predetermined tour of specific cities. Each show replaced another and was in turn replaced by a successor. Since the shows rotated like the spokes of a wheel, the circuit came to be known as a wheel. The eastern and western wheels improved the commercial organization of the industry and gave performers the security of forty weeks' employment for each season. In return for stability, the bureaucracy imposed uniformity on performers, material, and productions. Their policy of quality control and standardization of the product succeeded. Often, everything in a show appeared to be old because it *was* old: the jokes, the scenes, even the girls. A musical theater form is an organism, a living thing with a structure and functions peculiar to it. Block its growth and the organism atrophies. Before the fall, however, the *Brooklyn Eagle* reported on January 11, 1925, that the Columbia Amuse-

THE NIGHT OWLS

BIG BURLESQUE COMPANY

EXECUTIVE STAFF

ROBERT MANCHESTER . . . . Manager   JOHN DUNN . . . . Stage Manager
B. S. HODGES . . . . Business Manager   J. A. STROMBERG . . . . . . Musical Director

---

The Entertainment commences with a new and novel Burletta,

LORD FOUNTLEROY'S RECEPTION.

During which the following Artists appear:

MISS ANNIE WILMUTH,   MISS MAY ADAMS,
Vocal Selections.   Selected Ballads.

JOHN WILLS,   SAM BERNARD,
Conversation and Negro Melodies.   Burlesque Comedy with Songs.

Ending with a grand Operatic Medley, entitled the "NIGHT OWLS",
introducing the Lady Quartette,

MISSES NELSON, BLISS and LAPORTE SISTERS.

THE OLIO.

The Eccentric Comedian,

FRANK O'BRIEN,

In a new and original Black-face Idea, designed to make you laugh.

The Celebrated German Warbler,

MISS ANNIE WILMUTH,

In the Latest Successes.

America's Comedy Sketch Team,

John / WILLS & ADAMS, / May

In their latest Sensations, introducing Comedy Flashes.

THE OLD VOLUNTEERS,

By Misses Nelson, Keith, Bliss, Henderson, Vernon, Collings,
Von Beig and Storms.

ANNIE WILMUTH . . . . CAPTAIN

Rose / LAPORTE SISTERS, / Hilda

In their latest selections of Duets, Medleys, etc.

DELHAUER.

In his new Frog Act. The Greatest Performance of Modern
Times. The audience, astounded, laughed, and applauded for ten
minutes. The Frog's wonderful and funny piece of business
on an old Tomato Can on a Table to the Orchestra's melody
of "Rock-a-Bye Baby".

The inimitable,
SAM BERNARD.
The quintesence of quaint Comedians, Actors and Mimics.

Concluding with a new modern Burlesque, up to the times,
in THREE scenes, entitled
THE SCULPTOR'S DREAM; OR, LIVING MODELS
Libretto by Robert Manchester, Music composed and arranged by
Prof. J. A. Stromberg.
Produced under the direction of Robert Manchester.

CAST OF CHARACTERS.

Rudolph, the Sculptor . . . . Miss May Adams
Lord DeLille, a Polished Swell . . . . Miss Annie Wilmuth
Count Julian . . . . Miss Aggie Collins
Duke Rosbelle . . . . Miss Eva Drew
Prince O'Dare . . . . Miss Nettie Von Beig
Baron Vanecourt . . . . Miss Gertie Keith
Earl of Milton . . . . Miss Annie Harvey
Sir Paul Vargue . . . . Miss Mollie Henderson
King's Page . . . . Miss Etta Storms
Marguerite, in love with Rudolph . . . . Miss Hilda LaPorte
Lady Agatha . . . . Miss Roeme Nelson
Sabina Zambia . . . . Miss Louise Bliss
Lady Diana . . . . Miss Rose LaPorte
Maude Damurasy . . . . Miss Ray Vernon
Edith Lynn . . . . Miss Phoebe DeVere
Estelle Van Dette . . . . Miss Sophie Brown
The Slugger, a bad man . . . . Mr. John Wills
Simple Simon, a foolish boy . . . . Mr. John Dunn
Baron DeLaur, Marguerite's father . . . . Mr. Frank O'Brien
King Alphons . . . . Mr. Barrett Booth

NOTE—Please remain seated and witness our Living Statuary In Scene 3.

ment Company, the eastern wheel, entertained "an
average of 1,800 people a day in each of its 46 theatres.
This amounts to 70,000 daily and 500,000 weekly
throughout the circuit." **64**

"THE BLACK CROOK"

The characteristic elements that distinguished early burlesque derived from one successful, scandalous, and unsuspecting forerunner, *The Black Crook* (1866), a slight, undistinguished, and elaborately staged melodrama that featured more than one hundred ballet dancers exhibiting limbs in a spectacle that lasted for five-and-a-half hours. The initial run at New York's Niblo's Garden Theatre grossed one million dollars and contributed more to the public's growing interest in American musical comedy than any other single nineteenth-century production.

Ironically, *The Black Crook* was born of accident. When the Academy of Music burned to the ground, Henry C. Jarrett and Henry Palmer, sponsors of a French ballet troupe, desperately proposed a merger with William Wheatly who had commissioned a new melodrama for New York's Niblo's Garden. Although the original book did not make provisions for music or dancing, the French ballet was added as an adornment to the script which the producer had since come to regard with little

Costumes designed for the original production of *The Black Crook* (1866), the most successful musical of the nineteenth-century American musical theater. (Photo: Theatre and Music Collection, Museum of the City of New York)

enthusiasm. With an advance of $1500 to appease the offended author, an investment of $24,000 to refurbish the stage, and a production budget of $35,000, a theatrical event was manufactured that impressed the reviewers, shocked the clergy, and stunned the box office with unprecedented receipts. However questionable the value and skill of *The Black Crook* as theater art, it played in various productions from 1866 to 1929. Although its form did not approach the amalgam of book, lyrics, music, and dancing of a modern musical comedy, *The Black Crook* created a new audience for musical theater and demonstrated the potential of the book show at the box office. As *The Black Crook* became America's single most popular and financially successful musical theater production of the nineteenth century, it introduced to the world

Evangeline (1874) offered the public a musical score written specifically for the production. For the first time, the term *musical comedy* was applied to an American stage entertainment. (Photo: Music Department, Sheet Music Collection, Free Library of Philadelphia)

of musicals a large and important audience, discovered for the form a new self-respect, and mapped for future producers a new road to prosperity. The show launched one of the earliest show business spinoffs, the song "You Naughty, Naughty Men." Thereafter, the best of what was sung on America's musical stage was sung in the American home. Burlesque-spectacle-extravaganza established through its songs a connection between musical stage entertainment and everyday life. From that seed has grown much of what is most dear and beloved in our musical theater memories.

"EVANGELINE"

When *Evangeline* arrived at Niblo's Garden in 1874 as a "Picturesque Romantic Extravaganza," it added still another dimension to the growing accomplishment of the nineteenth-century musical: an original score. The score for *The Black Crook* was a *pasticcio,* but *Evangeline* greeted the public with new music. For the first time, a critic applied the term "musical comedy" to a stage entertainment. Critics found other virtues in *Evangeline.* The show projected an American tone, and it was clean, wholesome fun. As with the best work of Rodgers and Hammerstein, or Lerner and Loewe, *Evangeline* demonstrated that a solid show didn't need what a *New York Herald* critic called "the spice of vice" to be attractive to the public.

Comedy

The most consistent contribution of burlesque? Comedians. And no comedians were more innovative, influential, or astute than Weber and Fields. After a successful debut in burlesque with a "travesty" act, the team abandoned the wheels to open their own music hall, where they introduced a musical theater formula that combined a lavish musical show with an outrageous travesty of a dramatic show or melodrama. The critics agreed that the

67

Lew Fields, De Wolf Hopper, and Joe Weber in *Arizona*, 1900. The Weber and Fields formula combined a lavish musical show with outrageous travesty. (Photo: Byron, The Byron Collection, Museum of the City of New York)

Music Hall shows offer the public the best "musical comedy" available.

Weber and Fields began as a "Dutch act," a routine of old minstrel jokes delivered in a German accent. Weber played "Mike" and Fields played "Meyer." In fake chin whiskers, garish costumes, and formal derbies, they set out to amuse the public in the melting pot of the world. Fields was the heavy; Weber was the foil. On stage, the pillow-stuffed and padded Weber shouted, "I am delightfulness to meet you." Countered Fields, "Der disgust is all mine." Then came the slapstick. They prodded each other with canes, mopped one another across the floor, then concluded the act with a sure-fire knockabout sequence. The audiences roared. Routines like this became the model for broad burlesque humor.

Since the comedians of burlesque faced audiences daily in all parts of the country, they knew or were forced to learn the rudiments of comedy. In an article entitled **68**

"Adventures in Human Nature" published in the June 23, 1912, *Sunday Magazine,* Joe Weber and Lew Fields discussed the stage business that is indispensable to a burlesque act:

> The capitalizing of the audience's laughter we have set down in the following statistics, ranged in order of their value. An audience will laugh loudest at these episodes:
> 1. When a man sticks one finger into another man's eye.
> 2. When a man sticks two fingers into another man's eyes.
> 3. When a man chokes another man and shakes his head from side to side.
> 4. When a man kicks another man.
> 5. When a man bumps up suddenly against another man and knocks him off his feet.
> 6. When a man steps on another man's foot.
>
> Human nature as we have analyzed it, with results that will be told you by the cashier at our bank—will laugh louder and oftener at these spectacles . . . than at anything else one might name. Human nature here, as before, insists that the object of the attacks—the other man—be not really hurt.
>
> If a man . . . pokes his two forefingers into the eyes of another man without hurting them, then human nature will make you scream with mirth; not at the sight of the poking of the fingers into the other man's eyes . . . but because the man who had the fingers stuck into his eyes might have been hurt badly, but wasn't.
>
> The greatest laughter, the greatest comedy, is divided by a hair from the greatest tragedy. Always remember that!

Ideas languish without an appropriate and accessible forum for practice, performance, and evaluation. The burlesque system represented that forum for some of the most celebrated professional comedians of the era, one of whom was Ben Bard of the comedy team of Bard and Pearl. Like many of their innovative and enterprising predecessors, the team graduated from burlesque shows into more lucrative and respectable jobs in the Broadway revue. However, Bard never forgot his "old school" and what it taught him:

> [Burlesque] . . . was our college of humor, . . . a splendid training school. . . . We alone were responsible for our scenes. One of us would walk before an audience and say something, and the other would appear and answer it. It is really astonishing when you go back over the scenes that we worked up in this way. We started with only the dimmest general idea at all and in full view of the audience we developed the scene.

Women

Despite the comedians, many men in the audience came to see the notorious women who paid the price of personal scandal to stretch the boundaries of what audiences should be permitted to see on the musical stage. The female stars were hefty at first. Since a shapely turn-of-the-century female figure might easily weigh over 150 pounds, what the female performer exposed in tights was considerable. When she moved it was something to see! So burlesque management exploited the "Salome" dancers, the hula-hula dancers, "Venus" dancers, and audience participation exhibition. Miss Maurice Wood sang "Tickle My Fancy," then danced with a man in the audience. It was reported that Julia Sinclair did an audience participation exhibition during which "she [took] liberties with willing subjects." The more respectable houses offered soubrettes as an alternative to the dancers. Rather than cooch, shimmy, or disrobe, the soubrette sang, played scenes, offered imitations or double-entendre comedy routines.

Burlesque stars like Pauline Markham were featured in roles where provocative costuming would display the female anatomy to eager male audiences. (Photo: Theatre and Music Collection, Museum of the City of New York)

Decline

From the 1870s to the 1920s, bold, raucous, and gaudy burlesques toured the country playing to manly crowds eager for naughty, grown-up amusement. Nevertheless, they attracted respectable patrons to respectable theaters to see respectable performers. Today, *burlesque* is a dirty word sadly appropriate for the coarse and vulgar exhibitions of mechanical sexuality performed in rank and decaying theaters. What happened? *Variety* determined that the demise of the modest, old-style burlesque began around 1910 when the western wheel began giving "dirty" shows. The hip-grinding and breast-twirling of the featured cooch dancer led gradually to an entire chorus exhibition and eventually to burlesque shows of little else but bump and grind. The audience of the western wheel dissolved into stags and then into nothing. When the pattern repeated itself in the East, burlesque faded from consequence as a show business genre. However, the wounded god refused to die, choosing instead to undergo a metamorphosis into a more vulgar and lurid form. In the late 1920s, striptease replaced the naughty allure of the "hootchie-kootchie" with the desperate, jaded voyeurism of dispassionate disrobing. Not that the striptease was artless, totally. A good routine followed a definite form, included humor, and encouraged vocal audience participation. On the big-time Minsky circuit, the routine began with a "parade," a promenade around the stage by girls wearing anything from a gown and furs to a boa constrictor. Then came the "peel," the gradual removal of articles of clothing designed specifically for that purpose. Bumps and grinds accompanied the peel. The bump: a vigorous thrusting forward of the abdomen. The grind: an uninhibited twisting of the torso. A traditional finale called for the "flash," where the performer revealed herself for a minisecond completely nude except for a G-string. In the hands of an intelligent and ambitious artist like Gypsy Rose Lee, the striptease did indeed tease. Her act was of such style and class that it drove Miss Lee out of burlesque into a more lucrative career in the Broadway revue, film, and television. Most strippers were

71

On the night they raided Minsky's National Winter Garden Theatre in 1925, a certain Mademoiselle Fifi was reputed to have shed all her clothes. A self-described "classical barefoot dancer," Mlle. Fifi called her act "The Poetry of Motion." (Photo: Theatre Collection, Free Library of Philadelphia)

less fortunate. The tease degenerated soon into "show and tell" or, in the case of famous headliners, less revealing but more vulgar routines.

Burlesque abandoned its revered traditions willingly, but time, change, and a growing permissiveness in sexual mores proved just as responsible for its decline. As Bert Lahr, one of the leading comedians of the old-time burlesque, pointed out, there is more to be seen on the streets today in summer than was ever seen years ago on the burlesque stage. Just as the skirts were going up in everyday fashions, theater economics began to put the squeeze on the industry. At a time when principals in burlesque made about $90 a week, inferior comics received $250 a week in a Broadway revue or a touring 72 musical show. The comics who were the soul of the old burlesque deserted to star in the new and daring musical comedy. Without the best talent, the jokes, the routines, and the business got stale. Meanwhile, the Broadway revue initiated the fashion of displaying nude female bodies in respectable and "artistic" tableaus. Anatomical exposition became commonplace on the legitimate Broadway stage. The final indignity arrived gradually. As audiences dwindled, the old, worn-out theaters fell into disrepair, further neglect, and then rubble. No new theaters replaced the old ones. Where theaters survived, they were the oldest, dirtiest, and least valuable real estate in town. The theater is a place as well as an idea. The limitations of a playhouse go far to influence the limitations of the art practiced within. Sadly for burlesque, the place and the art fell apart simultaneously.

Musical comedy learned a lesson from burlesque, one the latter chose to ignore during its sad decline: Never abandon comedy. When the school graduates great comedians like W. C. Fields, Fanny Brice, Al Jolson, Abbott and Costello, Bert Lahr, and Sophie Tucker, you preserve the accomplishment and honor it. Critics issued warnings as early as 1869:

> The motive of burlesque is always satire. If this did not pervade it there would not be life enough in it to keep it sweet and make it hold together. The pleasure, the instruction and the comfort that we all derive from seeing the vices and the follies of others held up to ridicule are so great that we do not scrutinize too closely the manner in which they are conveyed. And in these days ridicule is, more than ever before, the sieve through which all men and things are sifted.

Without comedy, burlesque's fall from grace was swift and inexorable. A ruling by Boston Municipal Court Judge Charles Carr in a civil suit against a Boston burlesque theater in the 1930s summed up the form's final degradation:

> Burlesque has undergone great changes since Aristophanes and Sheridan. I put aside these book definitions and find that burlesque is among the lowest, if not the lowest form of production on the stage.

Extravaganza
and Spectacle

Paralleling burlesque in character and popularity were the extravaganzas, elaborate theater pieces loosely adapted from European models and offered to audiences as spectacles featuring female dancers brilliantly costumed, novel scenic devices, sumptuous settings, unusual lighting effects, and melodramatic musical scenes. There is no doubt that competing management used the names *burlesque, extravaganza,* and *spectacle* interchangeably, although the original distinction was that extravaganza and spectacle offered no satiric elements but were more inclined to fantastic material derived from mythology or fairy tale. In France, the *extravaganza* meant ballet theater evocations of fairyland. Although the English pantomime theater never became a popular form in the United States, the American extravaganzas borrowed many of its characteristic features, especially the awesome visual effects made possible by ingenious nineteenth-century theatrical machinery. During the Gilded Age, the public rushed to the theaters to marvel at the marvelous and witness the unbelievable. In 1868, Phillip Ripley wrote in the magazine *Public Spirit:*

> To be sure, in the most profitable and popular plays that now hold the stage, the poverty of the plot is only surpassed by the trashiness of the text; but the play going public, the people patronizing and paying for these plays, care nothing for the plot or text, since gorgeous costumes, the accompanying songs and orchestral music, the wonderful effects resulting from the management of calcium and other lights; the whole linked together in the mind's eye by bewilderingly long lines of limbs.

Grand fairy spectacles like *The Seven Daughters of Satan* personified this phase of the American musical theater. The program for Willard's Howard Athenaeum in Boston for February 3, 1866, credited mechanical effects and properties on an equal basis with scenery and costumes. It promised the audience a phenomenal spectacle **74**

Spectacles like Newton Beers' *Lost in London* catered to the popular taste for sumptuous scenery, gorgeous costumes, and awesome visual effects. (Photo: Theatre Collection, Free Library of Philadelphia)

replete with Grand Marches, Dances, and Choruses, concluding with the last Grand Scene, the Most Magnificent ever presented upon any Stage, representing the Birth of Cupid in the Bower of Ferns, produced at an immense out-lay. . . . Mirrors of Plate Glass are used, forming a Lake of Silver. Moving Fairy Cars, Revolving Gems, . . . concluding with the Magnificent Shower of Gold.

Later, the extravaganzas turned to native American themes as profitable subjects for spectacle. On December

10, 1893, the New Metropolitan Opera House presented Imre Kiralfy's "Grand Historical, Allegorical and Ballet Spectacle" *America*. For the price of a seat scaled from 25¢ in the family circle to a top of $1.50, the audience could expect to marvel at "Tableaux, Pageants, Marches, Groupings, Display and Choruses" illustrating "the Process of American Civilization During The Past Four Hundred Years In Its Many Varying Phases and The Advancement of Commerce, Science and Art."

THE HIPPODROME

When a symbol of the spectacle/extravaganza emerged, it was neither show, song, or performer, but—appropriately—a theater. Not just any theater, but a spectacular, colossal, extravagant behemoth of a New York theater called the Hippodrome. The brick, steel, and marble building resembled a large Arabian fortress as it occupied the entire block of Sixth Avenue between Forty-third and Forty-fourth streets. At capacity, 5200 customers had an unobstructed view of the floods and fires, elephant acts, water ballets, cavalry charges, and baseball games that made the turn-of-the-century public gasp in wonder. Architects designed the Hippodrome to unfold with ease even the most improbable theatrical spectacle. The dimensions of the stage measured 110 feet deep by 200 feet wide. Six hundred actors in simultaneous movement would not be uncomfortable on it. The stage floor could be raised or lowered at any of twelve bridges, while the stage apron could drop 14 feet and be filled by pumps circulating 150,000 gallons of water per minute. A favorite marvel repeated in many productions involved the mysterious disappearance of the entire chorus of female dancers which descended a glamorous stairway into the flooded orchestra pit. Of course, the clever architect provided concealed tubes of air for the mermaids until each could return to her normal element through escape routes under the theater. The opening night spectacle, *A Yankee Circus on Mars*, featured 280 female chorus dancers. Another production, *Andersonville; or, A Story of Wilson's Raiders* reproduced an authentic Civil War battle in which 480 soldiers clashed on stage. **76**

The opening spectacle at the New York Hippodrome, 1905. (Photo: Theatre and Music Collection, Museum of the City of New York)

Like burlesque, spectacle/extravaganza succumbed to rapid changes in public taste and theater economics. Billy Rose made an attempt to revive the Hippodrome with a spectacular production of Rodgers and Hart's *Jumbo* in 1935. The show was only a moderate success. Its closing ended the era of the Hippodrome. The real estate interest turned the theater into a basketball court, then demolished the building in 1939.

5

REVUE

The word is French. *Revue:* a satirical entertainment of fashionable Parisian life that features music, specialty acts, and pretty girls. In the American theater, the word applies to a similar form with American character and energy, a fast and lively nonbook show with musical numbers, comedy, sketches, and specialty routines. The basic ingredients of an American revue correspond to those in minstrelsy, burlesque, extravaganza, and spectacle. What makes the revue unique? How the ingredients are used. In a revue, a single unifying force organizes the variety of elements into a cumulative sequence of ascending theatrical peaks designed to service the concept of the show. The force can be a man (Florenz Ziegfeld), and idea (unionism), or an organization (the Theatre Guild). The concept behind the proceedings can range from the innocent exploitation of the physical beauty of the American girl, to the American labor movement of the 1930s, to an effort by the Theatre Guild Junior Players to raise money to buy tapestries for the new Guild Theatre. The revue brings unity to variety where before there was only variety. It stresses vital interrelationships among parts, the cumulative development of the program, and the overall effect of the production. Vaudeville valued sequence, but only in self-contained, independent acts. Interrelationships of minstrelsy were casual at best. The popularity of burlesque and extravaganza rose or fell on the strength of individual moments. It mattered only that there were enough spectacular moments to satisfy the **79** audience, not that those moments relate or develop in a necessarily purposeful direction. But a unified revue offers the artist of the theater many of the assets of a book show without their corresponding liabilities. Songs, dances, and scenes mounted within an evening's context accrue layers of meaning and feeling in performance unavailable when detached from material before and after. Context without the irreversible constraints of plot and character progression brings flexibility into the process of assembling a show. When a song doesn't work in Act I, try it in Act II, or substitute another song, or replace it with a sketch, and so on. Fueled by talent and creative energy, the options in a revue multiply. What is more, the flexibility they afford extends well beyond the rehearsal and tryout period. During the great era of the Broadway revue, management consistently upgraded their shows with new songs and sketches, even after the opening. Many revues were saved from box-office disaster by wise revision after the premiere—the most famous example being George White's first *Scandals.* Management revised successful productions, too, usually in an attempt to freshen up the show for a long run or a tour. When the Theatre Guild took the 1930 edition of *The Garrick Gaieties* on the road, the show was recomposed of new and old material. In order to stimulate business, gather publicity, and revitalize each performance, the Guild announced a new policy: "In each road city in which 'The Gaieties' is booked a contest will be held to secure a sketch on a local topic for which $100 will be paid to the winning author."

The revue borrowed its name from the French, but indigenous American musical theater forms gave it life, sustenance, and personality. The American revue is the child of four parents: minstrelsy—particularly the fantasia section where individual company members performed specialty routines; vaudeville—brief, self-contained acts of variety entertainment; burlesque—especially the model of extended satirical sketches; and spectacle/extravaganza—the artful blending of physical beauty with sumptuous or marvelous surroundings. These four parents produced an offspring with a dual personality. At times, the form exhibits a tendency to revert to the spectacular and populous manifestations of "eye-filling **80** display and rough humor" favored by the *Ziegfeld Follies* and the *George White Scandals*. Intimate revue identified the alternative personality, for the shows are of modest means, yet rich in charm, satire, and performance energy like *The Grand Street Follies, The Garrick Gaieties,* and *Pins and Needles.* Both personalities thrived in the receptive theatrical climate of the early decades of the twentieth century.

The Spectacular Revue

The earliest revues relied on the spectacle, beautiful girls, and wonderful stage effects that attracted an affluent public eager for glamour and excitement. The "spectacular" tradition originated with *The Passing Show* (1894), a lavish admixture of variety, burlesque, and travesty entertainment conceived as a topical extravaganza with inoffensive parodies. Contemporary critics responded favorably to the innovative potpourri of comedy, farce, drama, burlesque, *opéra bouffe,* and ballet, describing the form as a "musical-farcical-vaudeville entertainment" with "just sufficient coherency." Author Sydney Rosenfelt claimed that his show was a burlesque "review" of current events whose charm lay in its constant changes. Management claimed that the phenomenon was "something new under the sun." Both were correct, and the show started the trend for spectacular entertainments of constant change but with just sufficient coherency that came to be called revue.

"THE ZIEGFELD FOLLIES"

In the ensuing era of inflated incomes, overstimulated sensibilities, hedonistic pursuits, and escapist audiences, no theatrical phenomena emerged more appropriate to the times than the *Ziegfeld Follies.* A talented and flamboyant impresario named Florenz Ziegfeld produced

81

these revues in twenty-three editions from 1907 to 1931, with every edition dedicated to the principle of sumptuous spectacle punctuated for relief by specialty acts. Ziegfeld's formula for the revue called for (1) glamour, the glorification of the most beautiful American girls in settings of incomparable style and splendor; (2) pace, with all elements arranged to build toward two theatrical climaxes, the first-act curtain and the spectacular finale; (3) decency—"I pledge my honor that the American people will find nothing suggestive or unclean in my shows . . ."; and (4) spectacle. The closing number of Act I from the *Ziegfeld Follies* of 1927 involved fourteen pianos arranged along the ascending levels of a vast, semicircular staircase that supported two orchestras, one being a band of girl musicians called the Ingenues. Onto that set poured the unending flood of the full strength of the company, the feminine performers all costumed in shimmering white satin and yellow fringes and plumes.

Each year, Ziegfeld spent more money and energy to improve the newest *Follies* and raise its accomplishment above the standard set by the previous show. Ziegfeld detested aesthetic complacency.

> The public's about fed up on the usual run of revues and, if we're not careful, they're going to fight shy of the Follies. We've got to give them something out of the ordinary—something on a little higher plane than formerly, but with enough snap and go to it to prevent the suspicion of being high-brow. We'll let Ben Ali Haggin stage a couple of his gorgeous tableaux, turn Joseph Urban loose with a ton of paint and a battery of colored lights, commission Victor Herbert to write some of his most tuneful music and then get Irving Berlin, Gene Buck, Dave Stamper, W. C. Fields, Van and Schenck, Ray Dooley and the rest of 'em to supply the jazz and the laughs. In that way we ought to secure a production which will remain within the province of the Follies and at the same time be unusual.

This formula begat an institution so patent on the American scene that a Philadelphia critic observed:

> Why ask if it's good? Why ask how it compared with last year, or the year before or the year before that? Why attempt to classify it or criticize it? It's the typical Follies—colorful, tuneful, dazzling, alternately excruciatingly funny and satisfyingly beautiful—and there you are.

Ziegfeld engaged the most outstanding musical theater writers, composers, designers, and performers to execute his *Follies*. He commissioned over five hundred songs for the revues from composers like Jerome Kern, Victor Herbert—and Irving Berlin, the composer most identified with the *Follies* and its theme song, "A Pretty Girl Is Like a Melody" (1919). From the Viennese designer Joseph Urban, Ziegfeld accepted only the most magnificent sets, painted often in pointillist style. While earlier musical theater forms trained and developed star performers, Ziegfeld borrowed them. Through the casts of twenty-three editions paraded the show business celebrities of an age: Nora Bayes, Eva Tanguay, Fannie Brice, Ruth Etting, Marion Davies, Bert Williams, W. C. Fields, Ed Wynn, Eddie Cantor, Will Rogers, and others. Occasionally, the *Follies* launched a career, as with Lillian

Florenz Ziegfeld borrowed stars like Fanny Brice for his *Follies*. (Photo: Theatre Collection, Free Library of Philadelphia)

The *Follies* launched the career of Marilyn Miller, a beautiful dancer Ziegfeld groomed into "the most dazzling musical show personality of Broadway." (Photo: Theatre Collection, Free Library of Philadelphia)

Lorraine, Ann Pennington, and particularly Marilyn Miller, a beautiful dancer whom Ziegfeld groomed into the "most dazzling musical show personality of Broadway."

The *Ziegfeld Follies* declined gradually and through several stages. The brightest stars abandoned the revue after 1925, and Ziegfeld's main interest turned to book shows like *Show Boat.* The economic expense of mounting a *Follies* production skyrocketed from the initial cost of $13,000 for the first edition in 1907 to an estimated $289,000 for talent, stagehands, musicians, and equipment for the 1927 *Follies.* By 1930, the magic formula grew old-fashioned. The sketches maintained the old "tag-line-then-blackout" format, and predictable approaches replaced originality in song and dance. The gilded lily wilted. When Ziegfeld died in 1932, the spec- **84** tacular revue as a consistent and self-generating form died with him.

Florenz Ziegfeld was one of the greatest showmen produced by the American theater. He adopted the infant revue form and nurtured it skillfully into a magnificent and prosperous adult. He set the contemporary standards of style and luxury in decoration, costuming, and grand presentation, all of which he supported with the best that money could buy. He stimulated the business of and the audience for the American musical theater. Since every *Follies* production became the hot ticket with the box-office brokers, more than one hundred spectacular revues emulating the Ziegfeld touch opened on Broad-

The *Ziegfeld Follies* glorifed America and the beauty of the American girl. (Theatre and Music Collection, Museum of the City of New York)

way during the 1920s. In addition, Ziegfeld introduced musical theater planning and construction to Broadway when he commissioned Joseph Urban to design the Ziegfeld Theatre specifically for opera comique, musical comedies, and revues. The auditorium was constructed in the form of true ellipse, a procedure that eliminated all angles, enhanced the acoustics, and lent itself to a classic simplification in decoration.

In the best tradition of the American musical theater, Ziegfeld glorified America and the beauty of the American girl. Seldom in live theater entertainment have so many beautiful girls been assembled under one roof. His idea of success was this:

> I wish to make my work representative of America. I wish the girls in my productions to have the glory that is typical of the American woman, the spirit and ability. In all my productions, I strive to give the American composer, humorist and artist his chance. And to give a native quality to everything that I offer. There is nothing which the American, and especially the American girl is not capable of accomplishing. And my ambition is to give ample opportunities for the display of our best talent.

When Ziegfeld died, he cast a shadow over the entire land, not just the land of make-believe.

The Intimate Revue

Not all revues aspired to the spectacular. When *The Grand Street Follies* (1924) succeeded Off-Broadway, it instituted a new approach to the revue that rejected glamour and splendor for simplicity, wit, satire, and sophistication. These "intimate revues" placed imagination over budget, intellect over the senses, and originality over box-office formula. The essential difference between the spectacular revue and the intimate revue was less a matter of form and materials than one of tone and attitude. The intimate revue wore a daring demeanor made acceptable by the casual tone that accompanied all these **86** seemingly "unpremeditated" entertainments. Why unpremeditated? The earliest examples were just that. In fact, *The Grand Street Follies* became public amusement only when the management of the Neighborhood Playhouse, then the oldest active experimental theater organization in the United States, agreed to offer to its subscribers a show developed from the clever, in-house burlesques created for personal entertainment by some of the more inspired members of the playhouse organization. The public success of the first edition inspired a series of amusing and ingenious sequels that stressed an ensemble approach to a comedy of fearless satire committed by obscure players in an obscure theater. That model of joyous, witty, and charming musical entertainment initiated an alternative trend away from big-budget productions and produced a clutch of shows on and off Broadway that brought the revue before an even wider public. Many of the titles on the program for an early edition of *The Grand Street Follies* communicate the modest but satirical sense of the show (see page 88).

In order to succeed, an intimate revue requires clever sketches of comic impersonation, lively music, bright lyrics, and refreshing performances—ingredients the Theatre Guild Junior Players assembled for the Broadway production of *The Garrick Gaieties* (1925). In an intelligent, informal, and intimate atmosphere the show offered sketches that satirized Alfred Lunt and Lynn Fontanne, Calvin Coolidge, Ruth Draper, the American theater, Sidney Howard's *The Knew What They Wanted*, and The Three Musketeers. In the cast were Sterling Holloway, Libby Holman, and Lee Strasberg. Richard Rodgers wrote the music; Lorenz Hart wrote the lyrics. It was their first Broadway score. Another asset: the show cost only about $4000 or $5000 to produce. Richard Rodgers conducted the orchestra opening night. He was in an excellent position to assess the show and its reception. From his autobiography, *Musical Stages:**

> By now there was every indication that the audience was with
> us, and it wasn't simply because the customers were charitable

* From *Musical Stages* by Richard Rodgers. New York: Random House, 1975. Reprinted with permission.

THE NEIGHBORHOOD PLAYHOUSE

THE GRAND STREET FOLLIES

1. OPENING REMARKS
President of the Super-Drama League

2. PROLOGUE
(On Board the "S.S. Algonguin,"
Outward Bound for Three Mile Limit Bar)

3. "THE SHEWING-UP OF JO LEBLANCO"
A melodrama of wild frontier life among the cut-rates
of New York—according to Gee B. Pshaw
(Scene—Basement of Black & White's Drug Store)

4. NOT SO LONG, LONG AGO

5. SINFONICA DOMESTICA TRIANGULA
(Suite: Town and Country)
Performed for the first time by the ensemble of
The International Imposers Guild

6. "PLAY THE QUEEN"
or
"OLD IRISH POKER"
A medieval musical comedy awarded the first
Ignoble Prize as written by Poet Yeats and
performed by Strolling Players in Ireland
during the 14th Century
Showing unmistakably that there is nothing new
under the sun.

Intermission—20 Minutes

7. A BUSINESS CONFERENCE

8. "WHO KILLED THE GHOST?"
The Greatest Mystery Story of the Ages with this dazzling cast:

John Barrymore as Hamlet . . . . Albert Carrol
Fanny Brice as Ophelia . . . . Betty Prescott
David Warfield as Shylock . . . . Edgar Kent
Jane Cowl as Juliet . . . . Adrienne Morrison
Louise Closser Hale as Her Nurse . . . . Polaire Weissmann
Clare Eames as Lady Macbeth . . . . Florence Levine
Ghost of Hamlet's Father . . . . Edmond Rickett
Gallagher and Shean as the Grave-Diggers . . . . George Bratt and Junius Mathews
Valentino as the Player King . . . . John Scott
Pola Negri as the Player Queen . . . . Paula Trueman

9. AN ENGLISH FAVORITE

10. THE SOUTH SEA ISLANDS ACCORDING TO BROADWAY

11. A RECITAL AT THE TOWN HALL

12. EPILOGUE: THE VERDICT

toward the young or that the tickets were cheap. Though I couldn't see the people sitting in the dark behind me, I could actually feel the warmth and enthusiasm on the back of my neck. Our show was creating that rare kind of chemistry that produces sparks on both sides of the footlights. What the people were responding to was an irresistible combination of innocence and smartness.

How difficult it is to believe that *The Garrick Gaieties* score, and especially the song "Manhattan," premiered on Broadway years before *The Desert Song* and *The New Moon.* When Larry Hart wrote those lyrics, song words were the most underestimated and neglected component of a musical show. Contemporary lyrics either gushed

For *The Garrick Gaieties* (1925), Rodgers and Hart wrote their first complete Broadway score. (Photo: The Lynn Farnol Group, Inc.)

with ninteenth-century pseudo–German-romantic sentiment or merely assembled convenient clichés in forced
meters to accommodate a melody. So what if banal and
meaningless language polluted the theatrical air? went
the unstated argument: audiences came to hear the tune
and the vocalist had to sing *something*. Well, Larry Hart
didn't buy that, and he set his bright and cultivated mind
to the task of matching the composer's contribution with
language crafted into the homogenous, credible, and
functional unit we call a theater lyric. "Manhattan" became a hit song, launched the career of Rodgers and
Hart, and opened another avenue for the development
of the theater song. When a mutually supportive complement of words and music replaced the arbitrary matching
of word sounds to musical notes, the theater song acquired the potential for the mature expression of dramatic ideas. Because of *The Garrick Gaieties*, the American musical theater secured the lifetime service of
Richard Rodgers. Fortunately, the prospect of creating
the score for the show appeared just as the frustrated
and bitter composer was about to abandon his songwriting career for a $50-a-week job as a wholesaler in babies'
underwear.

Although the spectacular revues faded along with
American affluence during the Depression, the intimate
revue survived, especially as an effective forum for musical theater entertainments on serious subjects. The most
famous and successful thematic revue? *Pins and Needles*
(1937). Here was an intimate, satirical revue on the current labor movement filled with left-wing propaganda
and "shocking" material produced and performed by
members of the International Ladies Garment Workers
Union. The critics and the public measured the show
by the standards of professional revue production. The
consensus: "amazingly good." Like all great intimate revues, *Pins and Needles* marketed brains—in this case,
those of Harold Rome, the writer of sketches, music, and
lyrics who came to be called "a Noel Coward with a conscience." Some of his songs from the show, banned on
radio and by record companies because terms like *lockout*
and *arbitrate* were deemed too shocking for the public,
included "Doin' the Reactionary," "One Big Union for **90**

Two," and "Sing Us a Song with Social Significance." When *Pins and Needles* closed after 1108 performances, it set the record for the longest-running musical in New York theater history, a record unchallenged until another revolutionary success: *Oklahoma!*

The revue neither disappeared, adapted, or degenerated; it survives in cabaret, varsity shows, community theater, and an occasional New York production. We may appreciate the revue less for what it is, but we honor it more for what it did. First, the spectacular revue refined the use of spectacle for the modern musical theater. While the spectacle of burlesque and extravaganza overwhelmed by purposeful size and quantity, revue spectacle overwhelmed by beauty and taste. Second, intimate revue asserted the value of subtle, satirical comedy as an alternative to the rough, broad, and low comedy of burlesque and vaudeville. While a fully realized sketch may indeed employ a gag or a joke for a laugh, its nature and potential encourages experimentation with other sources of humor, namely, the true dramatic humor of character and situation. Third, the assembled nature of revue production stimulated the supply of new songwriters, many of whom could contribute simultaneously to a Broadway production. Some of the best songwriters of the early-twentieth-century musical theater worked in revues: Irving Berlin, Rodgers and Hart, Cole Porter, George Gershwin, and Harold Rome. Fourth, the competitive market for acceptable material of Ziegfeld caliber raised the self-imposed creative standards of writers, composers, and lyricists. When many artists respond to a genuine and widespread demand for a decent product, the market becomes alive, self-corrective, and open to all. Finally, revue taught the musical theater how to unify material. Wrote Leonard Bernstein:*

> Musical comedy has learned a lot from revues. It has learned to treat its book in the manner of a variety show; it has learned to take variety and unify it. This is one of the great secrets of

* From Leonard Bernstein, *The Joy of Music.* Copyright © 1954, 1955, 1956, 1957, 1958, 1959 by Leonard Bernstein. Reprinted with permission of Simon & Schuster, a Division of Gulf & Western Corporation.

our magic formula: to give an audience a continuous and convincing story, yet to have them leave the theater feeling that they have also had a rounded evening of fun—dancing, comedy scenes, emotional singing, gay singing, pretty girls—the works, but somehow all cleverly integrated into a good story. Variety in unity: that was the key lesson that musical comedy learned from the revue.

6

COMIC OPERA AND OPERETTA

Minstrelsy, burlesque, extravaganza, vaudeville, and revue burst onto the America theater scene in rapid succession without forcing the contemporary European forms out of the entertainment market. In fact, the rise of the indigenous forms paralleled a renaissance of European influence on the American musical theater. The popular French comic opera known as the *opéra bouffe* arrived in the United States first, when soon after the Civil War Jacques Offenbach's *La Grande Duchesse de Gerolstein* opened in New York to a favorable reception. Unlike the native American forms, the comic opera offered (1) a story with music that was more popular in tone than the music of serious opera, (2) spoken dialogue, (3) light subject matter, (4) comic interludes, and (5) a happy ending. What most impressed its admirers? Two qualities. The serious, artistic approach to the elements of the libretto (especially plot and characterization), and the music of composers of international stature. The European librettists introduced a frankness in dialogue and situation hitherto avoided in English-language musicals. The European composers set much of these lyrics to attractive and entertaining music that responded to valid dramatic considerations as well as the composer's need for a free musical imagination. In addition, the French companies were considered to have the best acting abilities and vocal prowess on the contemporary musical stage. The consistently high level of production and performance by these imported troupes gave the comic operas a twenty-year success that subsided only when eclipsed by a later passion for the English comic opera.

English Comic Opera

The American premiere of Gilbert and Sullivan's *H.M.S. Pinafore* at the Boston Museum, November 25, 1878, created a sensation. No imported musical theater entertainment up to that time had infected American audiences with comparable frenzy. Within one year, more than ninety *H.M.S. Pinafore* companies were touring the United States, five of them enjoying simultaneous success in New York City. Two features accounted for the unparalleled success of English comic opera. First was a libretto in the English language. For the first time since the ballad opera, American audiences could understand the dialogue, appreciate the jokes, and marvel at the clever rhymes in an imported book show without recourse to simultaneous translation. English lyrics helped an admiring public to learn the words, sing the melodies, and buy the sheet music. Second, the artistic integrity and careful crafting of Gilbert and Sullivan produced independent, completely realized scenes, lyrics, and songs that played on the stage as indispensable parts of an artistic and stylistic whole. The model of Gilbert and Sullivan provoked American librettists and composers into an immediate adoption of the form so that the production of musical theater pieces during the comic opera period (1880–1900) reached a volume unprecedented in American theater history. The American discovery of English comic opera signaled the start of musical theater in New York as a big-time, large-scale show business industry. By 1916, *Vanity Fair* reported a "fever" in New York that set "young men to whistling joyously the lively airs, . . . impelled young women to rhapsodic adoration of the feminine principals, and drew stage-door throngs of both sexes, such as never been seen before in America.

All Manhattan was comic opera mad."

Operetta

If we are to argue for the one moment when modern musical comedy identified recognizable parents, this would be it, because joining comic opera on the scene was a similar, even more influential form—operetta. Like comic opera, operetta employs music, spoken dialogue, light subject matter, comedy elements, and romance. The difference is one of emphasis and tone. Comic opera pursues its humors in a distinctly light and airy fashion. Delicate moments of romance intrude; they charm, and all is well. Operetta admits to greater ambition. It exploits all the ingredients of nineteenth-century romantic theater: love, adventure, color, music, dance, and all else that allows us to escape from our dull, everyday routine. Comic opera directs an appeal to the intellect; operetta gears its formula to the senses. In an exotic and picturesque locale, hero and heroine fall in love, suffer complications, reunite. Virtue triumphs; evil suffers; life imitates an all-consuming romantic fantasy. Where comic opera exploits plausible situations, farce, or verbal wit, operetta abandons everything to unfettered imagination. Early in the twentieth century, when lavish and melodic productions stroked a public eager for escapist entertainment, operetta enjoyed a temporary but spectacular success.

The form originated and developed in Germany and the Austro-Hungarian Empire during the final quarter of the nineteenth century. The most celebrated stage works of Franz von Suppe determined the genre; Johann Strauss and Franz Lehar perfected it. Fortunately, *Die Fledermaus* and *The Merry Widow* remain in the modern repertory, and the serious student of musical theater should attend a performance of one of these early models. Both hold the stage and suggest the roots of later American adaptations, the operettas redefined for American audiences by Victor Herbert, Sigmund Romberg, and Rudolf Friml.

VICTOR HERBERT

What survives today from the earlier periods of American musical theater? Only forms, memories of outstanding

Operettas like Victor Herbert's *Babes in Toyland* constitute the earliest major achievement of twentieth-century American music for the theater. (Photo: Byron, The Byron Collection, Museum of the City of New York)

performers, a few hit songs now in the folk song repertory, and an occasional scandal. Even the best minstrel shows, extravaganzas, burlesques, vaudeville shows, and revues defy revival. The operetta period launched by Victor Herbert marks an important step forward for the American musical because the shows and their songs survive and continue to occupy a permanent place in an active performance repertory.

Irish-born Victor Herbert composed the songs for *The Red Mill, Mlle. Modiste, Naughty Marietta, The Fortune Teller, Babes in Toyland,* and other operettas which constitute the earliest major achievement of twentieth-century American songs for the theater. For the ballads, comedy songs, choruses, and incidental music of his shows, Herbert cranked out the era's most beloved melodies, like "Kiss Me Again," "Ah, Sweet Mystery of Life," and "I'm Falling in Love with Someone." In his hands, the musical stage became the foremost forum for the beautiful, entrancing sounds demanded by the public. Aside from meeting demand, Herbert preferred tuneful music; he loved the lilt, the verve, and the harmonies.

It was said that he would play with these musical toys

Victor Herbert's operettas gave the audience music, not theater. In *Mlle. Modiste*, character, dialogue, plot, and situation existed only as accessories to song. (Photo: Byron, The Byron Collection, Museum of the City of New York)

as joyfully as a child plays with a doll, and his playtime produced music that appealed consistently to the majority. You could remember it; you could sing it; you could dance to it. Victor Herbert gave the theater audience music to take home and enjoy, and the theater audience was grateful. Note: Victor Herbert's operettas gave the audience music, not theater. The dialogue, plot, scenes, humor, and situations of his shows existed only as accessories to song. The story of how the composer came to write "Kiss Me Again" illustrates the dominance of song in the aesthetics of a Victor Herbert show. The melody was written by inspiration at Saratoga where the composer was giving a series of successful concerts. In the middle of his engagement, the librettist for *Mlle. Modiste* arrived with some ideas for his collaborator. Although the librettist offered no lyric or even an idea for a lyric, both agreed that an outstanding melody was needed for the prima donna to sing. A few nights later, a melody came to Herbert just before sleep. He arose, jotted down thirty-two measures, and went back to bed. Eventually, the librettist supplied suitable lyrics, and the song became **98**

"Kiss Me Again," the hit of the show. If Herbert sacrificed character and the dramatic functions of a lyric to music, he did so according to the accepted standards of the day. Undoubtedly, the man was a mature and talented musical craftsman, but one who worked in an immature musical theater. While his graceful tunes and simple harmonies adapted well to the operetta form, they sound better still when performed without lyrics or reference to dramatic context. Innovation and the perfection of the lyric-melody composite would come from others later. Herbert's destiny was to popularize the American operetta, consolidate its musical resources, influence the craft and instruction of musical theater orchestration, and reorganize the American theater orchestra for improved sound in performance.

SIGMUND ROMBERG

When American operetta reached the peak of critical and popular acclaim in the 1920s, the shows of Sigmund Romberg epitomized the form. Sigmund Romberg was born in Hungary, studied in Vienna, and emigrated to New York where he raised himself from a job in a pencil factory for $7 a week to a position as one of America's preeminent artists. Few composers have surpassed his seventy-eight shows and over two thousand songs. Like Victor Herbert's, Romberg's success thrived on "Old World" melody put to the service of romance and sentiment. Both men believed in the American market for European music and wrote accordingly. However, Romberg transcended his predecessor in one important respect: he understood the stage. Romberg saw in operetta a stage medium whose potential for the evocation of deep feeling increased in proportion to the skillful addition of great music. Where Herbert showcased marketable songs, Romberg marketed dramatic emotion through song. Not surprisingly, Romberg became the most celebrated American operetta composer to speak out on the importance of the book:

I have been endeavoring to have singing, dancing, comedy and a good cohesive story in one production, and to blend all these elements into one compact presentation which will not only please the ears and eyes, but also appeal to the intelligence of the playgoer. The book must be so arranged that neither dancing, music nor comedy must appear foreign to the action of the story.

Romberg's theories determined the procedures for his creative collaborations. Work at the piano did not begin until the author completed the book. Work on a song did not begin until the book provided a suitable dramatic situation. Unlike Victor Herbert, Romberg never indulged in musical "high spots" unless warranted by the story. These were but a few of the collaborative procedures devised by Romberg and Dorothy Donnelly for *My Maryland.* The overall process went something like this:

> We obtained the play *Barbara Fritchie,* on which it is based, and read it several times. Then Miss Donnelly went to her country place on Long Island to write the scenario and arrange the music cues. These cues indicate the logical places in which to interpolate songs. Also, with each cue she wrote down a number of suggestions for titles of the numbers.
>
> With some cues there were as many as twenty suggestions. I chose the ones I liked best and proceeded to compose the music. Usually, I wrote the opening phrase of the melody to fit the words of the title.
>
> When I had completed the score we got together and went over it to make revisions. Out of the eighteen numbers I had written we decided to retain eleven, discarding the rest. That meant I had to write seven new ones, which I did within two weeks. Again Miss Donnelly and I conferred and this time we agreed that all seemed satisfactory.

Romberg's concern for the text enriched his compositions. Here were theater songs within an operetta mode, songs that held the stage when performed in the context of the story. While the composer's job was to invent melodies and present them as a showman, Romberg knew that great music in the theater without acceptable dramatic context either wastes away or overwhelms the drama altogether. Consequently, he believed it to be his duty to create a complete score with mutually agreed-upon allegiance to the story well before the casting and rehearsal period. Lines could be cut or inserted during rehearsal, scenes and acts could be rewritten or dis- **100** carded. However, no such drastic corrective amenities were open to the serious composer. "If the composer hasn't done a good job at the outset, little can be done about it." These and other self-imposed standards and restrictions made it hard for the composer to write popular music for the theater. Often, he would write in the press how difficult it was to create simple melodies for untrained voices lacking the range of concert vocalists. He reasoned: "the smaller the range the less the composer has in the way of material to work with." Despite the limitations and the complaints, Romberg wrote, "Deep in My Heart" *(The Student Prince)*, "One Alone" *(The Desert Song)*, and "Lover Come Back to Me" *(The New Moon)*. Sigmund Romberg so extended the musical and dramatic possibilities of the operetta form that little soon remained to be said, sung, or explored. When American audiences abandoned operetta in the 1930s, so did Romberg.

RUDOLF FRIML

The last of the "Big Three" operetta composers was a serious musician (the student of Czech composer Antonin Dvořak), a renowned pianist, and the composer of thirty-three operettas. His name: Rudolf Friml. Contrary to his own protestations, Friml's musical theater world developed more in the direction of music than theater. Although he believed that music should support the action of a play as well as fit the personality of the character who sings it, Rudolf Friml's extraordinary career and reputation rested on a spectacular talent for musical improvisation that producers cultivated for the stage. At four, he astounded his native city of Prague by earning money as a prodigy at the piano. Years later, he would do the same in New York and Hollywood. The playwright and librettist Otto Harbach witnessed the phenomenon many times during their operetta collaboration.

> Friml cannot tell his own story in words. He speaks with the keys of the piano. When his friends . . . gather about him he usually goes to the piano and softly improvises as they talk. . . . If a significant sentence be spoken in words that touch the music sense of this master, . . . the composer springs to life. "Stop!"

he calls, "Let me try that." Then the words begin to take meaning in music under this magician's fingers.

Such blinding musical talent led the composer into creative procedures for the theater more attuned to those of Victor Herbert than of Sigmund Romberg. Complained Harbach:

> He is the only composer I ever heard of who always writes the music before he gets the words. All he wants—all he will listen to—is just a phrase. Give him a line that appeals and he is off—gone. You can't stop him. You can't read him the rest of it. You can't argue with him. As a matter of fact, you don't want to do anything but listen when he begins turning every facet of the thought into music, glittering with marvelous expression.
>
> The piano keys fly. Presently we catch just what we want. Then he is off again developing it. It is wonderful but it is hard on the man who has to write the words to fit the music. I know.

Friml's musical composition and improvisations never departed from the tradition that was his European musical heritage. He detested the new music of syncopated rhythms and dismissed the songs of the modern composers as "freakish, unmusical and exaggerated." For him, melody blossomed under his fingers and rhythm would never be allowed to get out of control. What an ideal talent and temperament for operetta! Consequently, *The Firefly* (1912), *Rose-Marie* (1924), and *The Vagabond King* (1925) achieved great success when Broadway audiences treasured musicals in the style of Viennese operetta that brought to the public such light music as "Indian Love Call" and "Only a Rose."

The model for operetta devised by the "Big Three" offered a wholesome story accompanied by melodic music, romantic settings, sentimental situations, and clean comedy—all wrapped attractively in a sumptuous production. Unfortunately, time eroded the acceptability of all but the music. From the splendid stories designed to quicken the pulse and soothe the emotions, time and change ripped away the romantic mask to reveal endless incidence of stereotyped characterization, undistinguished dialogue, senseless lyrics, and incidental humor locked into plots that are nothing if not contrived. While **102** the more insightful collaborators in operetta like Sigmund Romberg, Otto Harbach, and Frank Mandell valued the book in theory and practice, none was prepared to make music the ultimate servant of the play. Music was and is the greatest factor in operetta. The coauthor and coproducer of *The Desert Song*, Frank Mandell, wrote:

> The book is the cement of the operetta. And like cement, it must be used cunningly to hold the show together and fill in the cracks here and there. It is the wire on which the pearls of music and showmanship are strung. It shapes the color and entity of the show. And as a result, it is a very tricky thing to construct.
>
> As opposed to the book of a musical comedy which must be light and often the vehicle for a star, the book of an operetta must be solidly constructed, quick moving and reach the depths of tragedy and the heights of color. While there is always a hero and heroine, the book is written mainly for the story and not the cast. Humor is an important requisite and it must be effectively used. The story of a musical play is inclined often to be heavy. It is humor that balances it. The humor must be a particular kind. It cannot be topical as in a musical comedy. There can be no Broadway "gags." As a result most of the laughs are gotten through situations. The situation "gag" is not easy to write. It depends on a great many things as to how it gets over. Your comedian is an important factor as well as what precedes the situation. It is often on the reefs of those situation "gags" that a show is sunk. They are the trickiest portions of the book.
>
> It was Frederick the Great or some such emperor who said that the king was the first servant of the people. I define the duties of the book writer as the first servant of the musician.

When the librettist serves the musician, character, plot, dialogue, lyrics, situation, production concept, and humor suffer. Let's isolate two of those elements to illustrate the point. During a rehearsal of Victor Herbert's *Fortune Teller* in 1898, the stage manager approached an actor in the cast with what he decided was a brilliant bit of humor. Although the joke received a mixed reception among the members of the company, the stage manager persuaded an actor to try out the bit before an audience. He did. Uproarious laughter. The bit was retained in the book. Now, the masterpiece revealed:

I had a little bird and his name was Enza.
I opened the cage and in-flu-Enza.

If you've never encountered an operetta plot, you've never encountered plot at all! Sigmund Romberg placed *The New Moon* on an equal plane with *The Student Prince* and *The Desert Song* as his outstanding works. The plot of *The New Moon* follows the adventures of Robert Mission, a bondservant in New Orleans wanted by the police for opposition to loyal subjects of the king during the days of French rule in Louisiana. He is in love with Marianne, but duty demands that he lead the revolutionists against an unjust system. When Robert is captured and imprisoned in the ship *New Moon*, Marianne arranges for pirates to attack the ship and free her beloved. Eventually, all works out to a happy ending for the lovers. As you might suspect, people, time, and locale change in an opera plot. The plot itself? Changeless and eternal. For instance, the only variable in a Victor Herbert operetta is whether love will surmount temporary obstacles in Hungary, Paris, Holland, New Orleans, India, Afganistan, Persia, Lenz, or Ireland.

Decline

Rapid and enormous changes in American life during the late 1920s brought about the end of operetta. The mood of the Depression favored confrontation with new realities, not retreat into old-fashioned fantasy. In hardship and hope, America began to forge a new society— one that would soon stand poised on the brink of technological accomplishment and sophisticated living. When that public grew indifferent to nostalgia and sentiment, bored with storyland and impatient with obvious love situations, operetta was condemned to memory and occasional patronized revivals.

Ragtime and jazz surfaced, and the old quaint melodies lost favor. In their lifetime, Herbert, Romberg, and Friml came to symbolize a dead past while Kern, Rodgers, Berlin, Gershwin, and Porter rushed ahead into an exciting and dynamic future. The American popular song, like **104** the American musical theater which nurtured it, was ready at last for the final march toward maturity.

By then, the American musical theater tradition had embraced opera, ballad opera, *pasticcio,* puppet shows, pantomime, minstrelsy, burlesque, spectacular, extravaganza, revue, comic opera, operetta, and an adolescent musical comedy. In the following decades, experimentation, talent, courage, genius, and luck would weld the existing materials into a new form now recognized as characteristically American and universally identified as musical comedy.

It is time to shift our focus from musical theater forms to creative people. The future rides on the careers of those visionaries who drew deep from the well of tradition for the nourishment to reconstruct an art according to their convictions and lead the American musical theater into "the great period."

7

JEROME KERN

Early musical comedy fell into such a low creative state during the heyday of burlesque, vaudeville, and the revue that the critic Horace Wyndham complained, "I would defy even Sherlock Holmes himself to discover anything more utterly banal, pointless, devoid of humor, boring, silly, un-melodious and generally calculated to make one tired than the average musical comedy. . . ." Nevertheless, the box office for mindless book shows did such a booming business that inept showmen in progressively greater numbers rushed into the market to assemble pretty musical diversions guaranteed to please. In the hothouse atmosphere of limited talent and resources, imitation ruled the day, particularly in star vehicles—book shows designed exclusively to accommodate the unique gifts of celebrated performers. Here, precedent argued for the artistically intolerable practice of bypassing sound dramatic and theatrical means to achieve immediate commercial ends. Book, score, lyrics, dance, design, and performance served the star, the hit song, the quick laugh, and the favorite routine, and healthy profits vindicated producers who built and maintained theatrical empires on safe ideas, audience approval, and a distaste for risk. In an era when incredible texts, formula construction, imported laugh makers, and interpolated songs plagued the form, Broadway showmen mounted an average of forty to fifty musical shows each season. The American musical theater book show wallowed in a frighteningly prolonged and undistinguished adolescence.

109   Enter Jerome Kern, and with him the popular and

critically successful movement away from formula, spectacle, and commercial conservatism. Jerome Kern launched a theatrical revolution precisely when the popular musical theater needed to change. From the early modest forum of the Princess Theatre shows to the later stately surroundings of a Florenz Ziegfeld enterprise like *Show Boat*, Kern argued for, experimented with, and demonstrated in action the "principle of the book" from which the mature American musical play would develop. For too long a time in European and native forms, music dominated the musical theater. Despite his own considerable accomplishment of composing songs for over one hundred stage and screen productions from 1904 to 1945, Kern insisted throughout that a musical theater must be *theater*, an art form meant to be performed on a stage by actors who employ the elements of dramatic literature joined to song to reveal some aspect of human life. What gives form and substance to this art cannot be the expression of feeling in song, a mere component part, but rather something more complete, more all-embracing, more vital on which all the collaborators can build a unified artistic creation. What else but the play, the libretto, the text, the book? When Jerome Kern directed his considerable musical talent to accommodate this dramatic innovation, the American musical theater acquired a future as a unique cultural phenomenon with a rich aesthetic and an exciting potential.

What distinguished Jerome Kern from his predecessors was an attitude—specifically, a serious artistic attitude toward the philosophy and craft of creating for the musical theater. What had been mindless and frivolous entertainment represented to Kern a fertile field for exciting, important, and serious work. In collaboration, first with Guy Bolton and P. G. Wodehouse, and later with Oscar Hammerstein II and Otto Harbach, Jerome Kern set forth to discover how musicals (which were then assembled) could be conceived and written as works of art. If nothing more than for this spirit of artistic integrity, his example would have eventually rejuvenated the early musical stage. He did not stop there, however, because he went on to demonstrate how the book governs all things, that is, how the play generates the forces of music, **110** lyrics, design, and performance previously regarded as separate, departmentalized fragments glued together in rehearsal with enough attractive embellishments to conceal the cracks. These assumptions led to an intense and exclusive preoccupation with character, situation, plot, and dialogue in an era otherwise dominated by the shank and the buffoon. Here is a list of the contemporary antidotes for a weak scene, a dull moment or a creaky number: (1) Bring on the girls! (2) Hire the leading comic with his bagful of gags. (3) Reprise the hit song. (4) Rush in the star's specialty. Into this murky and hostile sea plunged a composer who held high some very curious thought and behavioral aberrations. Imagine. A composer with sound dramatic instincts and a far-reaching grasp of the theatrical medium who cared less about music than about story. Unbelievable? Jerome Kern claimed, "I am just a musical clothier. I can only write music to fit a given situation, character or lyric within a play or motion picture the way a good tailor fits a garment to a mannequin."

Contrary to the prevailing wish of composers who insisted on the separation of the musical sequence from dramatic problems, Kern insisted that song and book be joined throughout in a perfect and undistinguishable partnership. He deplored his peers who sat at the piano and allowed their ears to determine the value of a song. Jerome Kern became America's first great theater composer because he attempted to so immerse his musical talent in the characters of the book as to write songs for them alone. He believed the composer's mission must be to reveal character, thought, or feeling to the audience in suggestive musical images. When critics hailed his contribution at the expense of the libretto, the composer felt it was he who had failed. When reviews would pan the texts of Otto Harbach or Oscar Hammerstein II, Kern would rush to their defense in print. His argument: In a legitimate musical play, the merits of a score cannot be separated from those of the book or the show itself; the book conditions all the elements of a show regardless of how the critics respond to it. "Great score but lousy book." Humbug! The libretto sets off the score "just as **111** dark velvet makes a jewel shine brighter."

Despite his own protestations to the contrary, every Jerome Kern musical that navigated successfully the treacherous waters of Broadway did so mainly on the strength of its beautiful music. Time has not been kind to the ideas, plots, and dialogue of those librettos, but oh, those songs! Why do they survive pure and unblemished? Probably because a remarkable talent created songs that embodied simultaneously the finest elements of the "old" European and the "new" American musical traditions. Each song embraced comfortably the distinctively simple American style joined to the European light opera "feel" for glorious melody. If you sing, hum, or whistle, you can compare song melodies from each stage of Kern's career and experience in your own sound this special characteristic maintained throughout a forty-year period. Sound in succession "They Didn't Believe Me" (1914), "Look for the Silver Lining" (1920), "Make Believe" (1927), "Smoke Gets in Your Eyes" (1933), and "Long Ago (and Far Away)" (1944) and note how unchangeable was the work of this distinguished and inspired composer who fashioned novel melodic ideas, fresh harmonies, and subtly vigorous rhythmic variations into deftly crafted songs of timeless eloquence. Kern's secret, hallmark, and legacy are the same: the simple and direct musical statement. Within the traditional AABA or ABAB song patterns, the standard 2/4, 3/4, or 4/4 time signatures, and the typical thirty-two-measure refrain, Kern's talent exploded into theater songs of such freshness and light that a new lyricism emerged to fuel the dramatic needs of his theater, the popular music of the day, and the imaginative fires of future composers. Sound the melody of "I Told Every Little Star" (1932); do the same with a Richard Rodgers song like "Younger than Springtime" (1949) or "You Are Beautiful" (1958). Different melodies, to be sure, but each betrays the same character and tone of a distinct songwriting tradition sustained for over half a century.

Just as the style and quality of the songs influenced other composers, so did Kern's avowed dramatic purpose: to enhance the story without usurping dramatic priority. Since hit songs meant lines at the box office, the policy ran headlong against the prevailing currents in Broadway **112** musical production. Nevertheless, that inflexible attitude soon won over the critics, and what emerged was a more fluid and compact union of song and story. Many called it the new musical comedy; in reality, it was a new form, the musical play. In it, every song had a rightful place in the story. Within the book, no elements were intended to function without the others. Never was audience reaction a target in creation or performance. Character, situation, mood, and theme were placed ahead of hit song, star, gags, and formula. To weave music deeper into the fabric of the musical drama, Kern drew on the example of the "leitmotif" theory from opera composition. The songs that were once adjacent to or companions of the drama now became an essential part of the drama. Music began to personify character, foreshadow mood, echo emotion, underscore dialogue, and parallel the libretto's emerging patterns of action and rest. And to think it all began at the Princess Theatre.

The Princess Theatre Shows

Jerome Kern commanded the musical comedy revolution from the Princess Theatre in New York City, where he launched such innovative shows as *Nobody Home* (1915); *Very Good, Eddie* (1915); *Oh, Boy!* (1917); and *Oh Lady! Lady!* (1918). Working mostly in collaboration with Guy Bolton (book) and P. G. Wodehouse (lyrics), Kern set sail for uncharted territory. What he discovered was a precious, valuable, and entirely new species: the intimate, simple, adult, intelligent, economical, small-cast musical show. Surrounding these rare and special creatures were untold resources of American subjects, characters, and situations ready to be brought back for American audiences. At last, the popular musical stage discovered a genuine alternative to the tired conventions of romantic escapism embodied in the operetta, the spectacular revues, and the Broadway star vehicles. How were the Prin-

Jerome Kern commanded a musical theater revolution from the Princess Theatre where shows like *Very Good, Eddie* (1918) presented American subjects in simple, economical, small cast productions. (Photo: Theatre and Music Collection, Museum of the City of New York)

cess Theatre shows a genuine alternative? They gave the American audience a dramatic stage experience comparable to their own. When these shows bridged the chasm between stage life and real life, the American musical theater moved closer to its public than ever before. It would be inaccurate to say that the Princess Theatre shows introduced realism into the American musical stage. However, they did demonstrate the stage power of a natural treatment of everyday people and situations in popular art. A popular and important art must be able to reach out and speak to all people and make them think and feel as it transforms them. The Princess Theatre shows deserve our attention because they put the book show tradition on the road to pulling audiences back into themselves and their emotions at a time when the major- **114** ity of showmen launched spectacular escapist assaults on audience sensibilities. The Princess Theatre shows rediscovered the enormous energy stored in the simple American musical of, from, and for the people, then kept alive that unique style in a body of work billed by their knowing creators as musical farce "of a kind that's different."

Fortunately, talent, intelligence, and craft supported the innovations of these shows. So did sound artistic methods. The collaborators rejected the conventional process of assembling the parts of a musical show for the more dramatically sound concept of integration, that is, the tight interaction of book, score, lyrics, dance, design, and performance placed in the service of the story's natural development. The Princess Theatre shows excelled in two important areas of musical theater integration: comedy and lyrics. The comedy in the early musicals was generated by hired comedians. Jokes, gags, pratfalls, and slapstick applied indiscriminately forged an awkward comedy, extraneous to the story, inconsistent in effect, and always difficult to sustain. Even the best efforts of the most resourceful comedians served to interrupt the dramatic development of the book. The Princess Theatre shows aimed for humor that flowed directly from believably funny characters put into a logical succession of laughable situations. Where overvalued lyricists cranked out graceless patchworks of sentimental, overblown phrases bound by diction too "literary" to approximate the sound of spoken language, P. G. Wodehouse crafted lyrics free from clichés, predictable rhymes, obvious subjects, and forced meanings. The harnessed intelligence of a witty person dedicated to originality in self-expression brought something exciting to what was then the most neglected element of musical theater collaboration. The lyrics survive—clean, light, smart, fresh, precise, and theatrical. While Kern and his collaborators inherited a musical theater so dominated by the tune that words needed only to provide acceptable vowel-consonant patterns that reflected that melodic phrase, they passed on a more sophisticated model to the emerging craftsmen of the 1920s. What they began at the Princess Theatre

would continue in Kern's mature work with other partners, the best of Rodgers and Hart, some Gershwin, late Porter, and all the mature and integrated musicals of the golden era of the forties and fifties.

"Show Boat"

If Jerome Kern contributed no more than the Princess Theatre shows, he would retain a reputation as the outstanding pioneer of early musical comedy. However, the ideas, talent, skill, and dramatic sensitivity responded to a greater challenge and secured an even greater accomplishment in *Show Boat* (1927), the foremost critical and popular achievement of the musical theater of the 1920s. What a distinguished collaboration! Oscar Hammerstein

Jerome Kern wrote the music for *Show Boat* (1927), the foremost critical and popular achievement of the musical theater of the 1920s. (Photo: The Lynn Farnol Group, Inc.)

II wrote the lyrics and adapted the book from the Edna Ferber novel, and Florenz Ziegfeld produced the show. Jerome Kern did more than compose the score; he functioned on all levels of theatrical collaboration. When Edna Ferber expressed grave reservations about the suitability of her novel for stage entertainment, it was Kern who assured her that the project would avoid the inanities of the contemporary light musical stage and concentrate on a new and dramatically sound theatrical expression of the deeply human values that were worked into the original material. To accomplish this objective, Kern and Hammerstein agreed to make all the musical and dramatic elements of a book show evolve organically from the spirit of the novel. Nothing was permitted to interfere with the integrity of the process or the power of the original concept. Consequently, the show came to the stage as fresh and strong as it was triumphant, more a musical play than a musical comedy, the only musical show of its time to achieve a drama that could withstand comparison with a "legitimate" play. Richard Watts, Jr., in the *Herald Tribune* praised the splendid production, the "lovely" and "intelligently melodic" score, and the "sturdy" libretto. The *New York Times* singled out the book, lyrics, and score for exceptional praise. The prototype for the serious modern musical had arrived.

THE SCORE

Oscar Hammerstein II and his libretto for *Show Boat* drew from Jerome Kern one of the most dramatic and consistently melodic scores in the popular lyric theater repertory. In a time when musicals could sustain a smash-hit run on the strength of one hit tune, *Show Boat* offered "Can't Help Lovin' dat Man," "Bill," "Ol' Man River," "Make Believe," "Why Do I Love You?" and "You Are Love," among others. More impressive than the beauty and strength of the score as a whole is the maturity of form and style in each of the songs. By 1927, the musical structure of the American popular song crystallized into the AABA form which gives the listener the pleasure of recognition by returning to the original thematic material. For example, in "Ol' Man River" the principal melodic motif runs for eight measures beginning on the word *Ol'* and ending on the word *along.* The melody repeats for another eight measures beginning on the word *He* and ending on the word *along.* A contrasting melodic motif interrupts the repetition with an eight-measure release beginning on the word *You* and ending on the word *jail,* only to return to the final repetition of the original melody of eight measures beginning on the word *Ah* ("I"). Both the AABA song structure and its subtle variant ABAB represent outlines for mature song construction, that is, form of sufficient breadth of composition to permit an ambitious expression of drama through music, yet disciplined enough to contain the song for natural integration into the broader framework of the show. As the public recognized no difference between show songs and the "pop" songs, Jerome Kern was able to filter through *Show Boat* fresh and attractive music that responded to the taste of America only after it embodied dramatic or theatrical purpose in design or melodic content. He wrote no more popular and enduring a song than "Ol' Man River," a dramatic statement in music where the design of the melody, the character of the musical phrasing, and the nature of the harmonic accompaniment reflect always the dual images of the song's dramatic purpose. Note how the developing succession of musical phrases reflect the increased intensity of the vocalist's lyric by climbing steadily in melodic intervals until the explosive climax at the conclusion of the song. Here Kern demonstrated how musical development can and should parallel the development of the song's idea. Note how the slow and somber repetition of the initial note in the refrain becomes a recurrent melodic figure that projects the strong and somber statement of the lyric, and how often the composer repeats or inverts the technique to sustain in sound the song's dramatic character. Within the first eight measures of the refrain, the powerful repeated-note motif appears in the first, second, third, fifth, and sixth measures, after which the entire process repeats in the second and final A of the song's AABA form. As a dramatic complement to this technique, Kern chose an arpeggio figure to accompany the melody and add an aural suggestion of the deep flowing quality of the Mississippi River. **118**

By sounding the notes of a chord in rapid succession instead of striking the notes simultaneously, the instrument produces a rippling effect not unlike the image of waves or similar movements on the surface of water. The score for *Show Boat* opened up a world of new creative directions for the serious musical theater.

THE BOOK

Oscar Hammerstein II fashioned a book for *Show Boat* that brought before the public for the first time the human and moral concerns that would become the heart of the enduring American musical. The collaborators built *Show Boat* around the concept of an adult musical show where plot, character, and situation dared the direct and uncompromising treatment of social issues, none more genuinely felt or aggressively written than in the scenes for the poor and exhausted southern Negro. Almost without exception, the American theater treated the black person as a comic character in the genre of fool, clown, or "darkie" simpleton. The race was victim of much that was tasteless and derisive until *Show Boat* revealed a sympathetic treatment of a serious dramatic situation where dignity survives, where misery, hard work, and suffering waste the body but not man's indomitable spirit. *Show Boat* originated a new type of musical book called the musical play, a form that is neither opera, comic opera, operetta, musical comedy, or straight play with music. In the musical play, the audience senses a distinct personality achieved by certain attributes. First, the musical play invites the audience to take story, characterization, and performance seriously. Usually, the book eschews an entirely light and frivolous content for an admixture of comic interludes between serious or tragic incidents. Second, the musical play unfolds through dialogue that approximates the sounds and rhythms of natural speech. Musical comedy dialogue trades on the glib, brassy, "always-on-stage" quality that comes from lines with excessive wit, jokes, or "zingers." Operetta dialogue pursues the opposite extreme, broadly sentimental, pseudopoetic, unreal, and remote expression. Third, the musical play organizes everything around an interesting, well-motivated story. Lyrics, songs, and dance carry the story forward and are never interpolated for diversion or effect. Since the book must never stop moving forward, the elements of a musical show must express as well as develop the story in a smooth and linear dramatic progression.

THE LYRICS

While the published sheet music of "Ol' Man River" read "Words by Oscar Hammerstein II," the polish, craft, grace, and depth of feeling in those words signal more than mere word juggling: they are the major work of a master lyricist. Note the relative strength of the untraditional verse when compared to the refrain. The song lyric is of one piece but in two valuable sections, so unlike the contemporary procedure of an obligatory but weak lead-in verse followed by a strong refrain. Note the phrase progression in the refrain that pushes the thought along with the same momentum built by the composer into the restless flow of the notes. Note the colloquial and uneducated flavor of the language sounds achieved by approximate aural spellings like "dere" for "there," "dat" for "that," and "de" for "the," while not one phrase in the entire lyrics eludes immediate understanding by the listener. Note the purposefully conspicuous absence of forced rhyme or the boxed and metered phrases that would reduce the loose and open construction of the song to a tight series of predictable schemes. Above all, note the daring and uncompromising content of the lyric and remember its date: 1927. Beyond all human and technical accomplishment, the lyric points to a new role in musical theater that Hammerstein would explore more fully in his work with Richard Rodgers: the lyricist as lecturer-philosopher-educator. The *Show Boat* lyrics mark the beginning of the end for the epithet "Words by" as a valid working description of the function and responsibility of the serious composer's equally serious collaborator.

While the end of the 1920s represented a turning point for the American musical theater with *Show Boat* as the crucial pivot between past and future, Jerome Kern did not move forward with shows like *The Cat and the Fiddle, Music in the Air,* and *Roberta.* As he stepped **120** forward into the first rank of American theater composers, the shows didn't follow. The talent, craft, and ideas that broke new ground in previous generations returned to cultivate such familiar territory that critics and audiences resumed the old habit of embracing his shows for melodious scores that rescued weak librettos. In 1939, the composer abandoned Broadway to pursue a Hollywood career that lasted until his death in 1945.

While contemporaries like George Gershwin and Cole Porter monopolized the public limelight, Jerome Kern worked for over three decades to draft the plans for a serious and mature American musical theater. He was a rare phenomenon: a talented composer with an innate feeling for dramatic lyrics, character, story, and style. When Kern left Broadway, the royal line of succession passed to Rodgers and Hammerstein, and through Hammerstein to Stephen Sondheim, all of whom inherited the following crown jewels:

1. An American musical theater built on the primacy of the text.
2. An ambition and commitment to write good music for good theater.
3. A determination to compose one's own music regardless of book, style, or locale.
4. A disciplined method of creation devoted to tireless exploration and meticulous craftsmanship.
5. An uncompromising creative spirit.

When Jerome Kern died, all America paid tribute. However, no praise was more appropriate than the simple words of Richard Rodgers, who wrote in his biography, *Musical Stages:**

> No matter what I myself accomplished, I always felt I was continuing to build the same kind of musical theater that Kern had helped to create.

* From *Musical Stages* by Richard Rodgers. New York: Random House, 1975. Reprinted with permission.

RODGERS
AND
HAMMERSTEIN

When Cole Porter was asked to name the most profound change in musical comedy during his lifetime, he replied, "Rodgers and Hammerstein." The collaboration of Richard Rodgers and Oscar Hammerstein II was established in 1942 and lasted until Hammerstein's death in 1960. It produced nine musical plays—*Oklahoma!* (1943), *Carousel* (1945), *Allegro* (1947), *South Pacific* (1949), *The King and I* (1951), *Me and Juliet* (1953), *Pipe Dream* (1955), *Flower Drum Song* (1958), and *The Sound of Music* (1959)—the film *State Fair* (1945), and the television musical *Cinderella* (1957). It was an ideal creative partnership. Both men respected talent and craft, shared similar social habits, and saw the world from the same musical viewpoint. They grew up in the same theater milieu, responded to similar influences, and participated in the same currents of artistic thought and activity. Each was a distinguished veteran of musical theater at the beginning of their collaboration, having created a combined total of fifty-nine shows between them. Under their gentle but knowledgeable guidance, the American musical theater would develop into one of the most satisfying and unique American contributions to theater.

Hammerstein before Rodgers

Oscar Hammerstein II was born into a theatrical family and committed himself to the theater despite all efforts of the family to discourage him. When he was old enough to handle a job in the family theatrical empire, he abandoned himself to his duties totally, and in the process assimilated much about play production and the duties of the theater artist. During this period, Mae West took Oscar aside one day and advised, "Get out of the theater, kid, and go back to law. You've got too much class to hang around the stage." He didn't take the advice. Soon after, Oscar as lyricist teamed with author Otto Harbach and composer Vincent Youmans for *Wildflower.* Under the friendly and competent guidance of Harbach, Hammerstein began to create professional material for Broadway's musical stage.

Regarding these early successes, Hammerstein was fond of saying that he was born into the theatrical world with two gold spoons in his mouth, one spoon being Uncle Arthur Hammerstein, who took him into his producing organization, and the other being Otto Harbach, who accepted him as a collaborator. In 1949, Hammerstein wrote the following benediction to Harbach into the "Notes" which preceded his book *Lyrics:**

> His generosity in dividing credits and royalties with me was the least of his favors. Much more important were the things he taught me about writing for the theater. Otto is the best play analyst I have ever met. He is also a patient man and a born teacher. Like most young writers, I had a great eagerness to get words down on paper. He taught me to think a long time before actually writing.

Also:

> He taught me never to stop work on anything if you can think of one small improvement to make. To speak of his nonprofes-

* From Oscar Hammerstein II, *Lyrics.* Copyright © 1949, 1977 by Oscar Hammerstein II. Reprinted by permission of Simon & Schuster, a Division of Gulf & Western Corporation.

sional qualities as a civilized human being is completely irrelevant to these notes. Please, nevertheless, let me record that he is the kindest, most tolerant and wisest man I have ever met.

Through Otto Harbach, Hammerstein was led into collaboration with Jerome Kern for *Sunny*, an elaborate vehicle for Marilyn Miller. After that, Hammerstein turned to Herbert Stothart and George Gershwin as collaborators for *Song of the Flame*, but the result was a formless work that was neither good operetta nor good musical comedy. It is important to mention that show because Oscar's experience with it led him to concentrate on operetta as a form consistent with his aims of integrating elements of musical comedy with opera. Writing from this perspective, he was able to achieve new standards for success in his career with two very romantic, pseudo-European shows, *The Wild Rose*, with music by Rudolf Friml, and *The Desert Song*, with music by Sigmund Romberg.

For these operettas, Hammerstein wrote the lyrics for the songs after the music. For over twenty-five years, he fit words to the notes of Jerome Kern, Herbert Stothart, Sigmund Romberg, Rudolf Friml, George Gershwin, and Vincent Youmans. In his "Notes" to *Lyrics* he explained that it was easier to write a lyric to fit a composer's melody rather than force some Middle European or Viennese composer to understand the subtle complexities of the English language. Besides, the influence of ragtime and jazz made it profitable to allow the composer maximum freedom from the possible limitations of strict and rigid meters. Furthermore, the hit melodies of the moment had to be good dance melodies. The lyric writer was necessarily relegated to a position well behind that of the composer and so forced to fit words to a refrain written mainly to be danced.

By 1927, Hammerstein had achieved the technical skill that allowed him to provide a composer with a functional book and lyrics. This skill found its fullest expression in *Show Boat*, the first modern American musical play. It was here that Hammerstein first indicated his potential for greatness. A human concern for the content of Edna Ferber's novel as well as a sound respect for its style 125 led him to write a book and lyrics that revealed to audi-

PIERRE: "Margot, you don't mean to say you are beginning to love that cut-throat, that ruffian?"

For operettas like *The Desert Song*, Oscar Hammerstein II wrote lyrics to fit a composer's melody. (Photo: The Lynn Farnol Group, Inc.)

ences something of the moral concerns of the author and of what American musical comedy might become.

Of *Show Boat* Richard Rodgers has said, "I think it was the deep impression this piece made on me that sent me to Oscar years later with the suggestion that we might find it advisable to work together." Indeed, many of the elements that would characterize their collaboration were evident here. At best, *Show Boat* reflected Oscar Hammerstein's capacity to reject formula in the search for an adult musical theater form. Here **126**

Hammerstein wrote the book and lyrics for *Show Boat* (1927), the first modern musical play. The wedding scene is from a 1946 revival. (Photo: The Lynn Farnol Group, Inc.)

was plot, situation, and characterization that dared be believable. At the forefront was the author's concern for the poor southern Negro. In *Show Boat*, sympathetic treatment revealed a situation in which dignity survives, in which misery, hard work, and suffering attack the body but not the soul. Hammerstein would contribute more commentary on racial prejudice after *Show Boat*, but that first effort still holds up when we reflect on the nature and preferences of those earlier audiences for light American musical entertainment.

Despite the promise of *Show Boat*, Hammerstein was unable to produce works of comparable success during the period from 1928 to 1940. With *The New Moon*, he returned to operetta. Then eight "musical comedies" followed and failed. Among the forgotten shows in American musical theater history which bore the "Hammerstein touch" were *Free for All, East Wind, Three Sisters, May Wine, Gentleman Unafraid, Glorious Morning, American Jubilee,* and *Sunny River*.

127

By 1941, it had become apparent that except for *Show Boat,* Oscar Hammerstein II had not succeeded in creating a celebrated body of work outside the operetta form. In attempting to make the musical theater advance to a more complex, quasi-operatic level, he only effected a return to the form of theater—operetta—that *Show Boat* had helped to make obsolete.

Rodgers before Hammerstein

Although Richard Rodgers was not born into the theater, his family made him aware of the world of musical theater at an early age. Rodgers's earliest memories are of his parents singing the complete vocal scores from the latest musical comedies.

> Once they had attended a given musical show, the printed score would be brought home and placed on the rack of the upright piano in the second-floor living room. Thereafter, in the evenings of the ensuing two or three weeks (barring calls from patients who were tactless enough to need night visits), Mrs. Rodgers, looking over her shoulder, would sing. Together, they would go through the entire score, from opening chorus to finale.*

By age six, Rodgers had taught himself to play the piano with both hands. Since his parents were both proud and delighted with that feat, Rodgers was given piano lessons and encouraged from the start to seek a career in music. Rodgers has always been grateful for his parents' unwavering moral and financial support during his early years.

Rodgers's dedication to the theatre also began early in life. His first theatrical experience, the musical *Pied Piper,* elicited an emotional response that has been kept intact in the composer's memory. "The moment the curtain went up I was carried into a world of glamour and beauty I had never known existed." From that moment

* From *Some Enchanted Evenings* by Deems Taylor (New York: Harper and Row Publishers, Inc., 1953). Used with permission.

on, "life for me began on Saturdays at two-thirty," and the "Saturday experience" was often repeated, since Rodgers's parents and grandparents attended the Saturday matinee downtown or at the 125th Street Theater. The Kern-Bolton-Wodehouse musicals made an impact on him during this period.

The Princess Theatre Shows—*Nobody Home; Very Good, Eddie; Oh, Boy!; Oh, Lady! Lady!*—and another work from the same period, *Leave It to Jane*, were fresh, new, and represented a genre of American musical comedy based on a simple, natural, and direct approach. Jerome Kern's contribution cast a spell on the stagestruck youngster. Rodgers would later say:*

> The influence of the hero on such a hero-worshiper is not easy to calculate, but it was a deep and lasting one. . . . I have never felt that enough has been said about Kern's contribution to American music through his influence on subsequent writers of music in this country.

Rodgers was about nine years old when he began to sit at the piano for hours at a time and compose melodies of his own. Soon after, he learned to put his musical thoughts down on paper by a patient process of trial and error. Armed with a notation system at fourteen, he produced his first two complete songs, "Campfire Days" and "The Auto Show Girl." While attending DeWitt Clinton High School, Rodgers wrote the scores for two amateur shows, *One Minute Please* and *Up State and Down*, after which Phillip Leavitt persuaded Rodgers to seek out a lyricist and initiate a steady and professional song-producing arrangement. It was Leavitt who suggested that Richard Rodgers contact Lorenz Hart, an "extremely cultured" Columbia graduate who "devoured great literature, could quote Shakespeare by the page, was a passionate theater goer . . . was a lover of good music and opera," and "who had high hopes of becoming a writer." A meeting was arranged for a Sunday afternoon in 1918 at Hart's brownstone apartment. The creative union was immediate. Hart admired Rodgers's easy gift

* From *Richard Rogers* by David Ewen (New York: Holt, Rinehart, and Winston, 1957). Used by arrangement with the author and his agents, Scott Meredith Literary Agency, Inc.

for pleasing melody; Rodgers admired the refinement and good taste of Hart's lyrics. When Rodgers left 119th Street that afternoon, he had acquired, in his own words, "a career, a partner, a best friend—and a source of permanent irritation."

RODGERS AND HART

Richard Rodgers and Lorenz Hart produced their first complete score for a Columbia University Varsity Show, *Fly with Me*, the first time that the work of a freshman had ever been accepted by the approval committee. Hart, an alumnus of Columbia, was eligible to write for the Varsity Show, an annual production which ran for a week at the Hotel Astor ballroom and used a professional orchestra. When Rodgers was once asked why he chose Columbia rather than any other college, his reply was simply, "The varsity show. . . . What better incentive could you have for going to college? Lew Fields attended one of the performances of *Fly with Me* and announced his intention to use some of the songs in his next Broadway musical, *Poor Little Ritz Girl*. Although only seven of the fifteen numbers in the show were his—the others were by Sigmund Romberg—the production initiated Rodgers into the world of Broadway musicals. Rodgers and Hart had a partial responsibility in a modest success; their career was launched in a positive fashion, with author Fields publicly and prophetically expressing his enthusiasm for the young composer: "Rodgers has real talent. I think that within a few years he will be in a class by himself."

The collaboration of Rodgers and Hart lasted from 1918 to 1943 and produced twenty-seven stage musicals and eight motion picture scores. Together, they created nearly one thousand songs, seventy-five of which are frequently played today. Of their first seventeen shows, from *Garrick Gaieties*, sponsored by the Theatre Guild, to *America's Sweetheart*, seven were major successes and ten were failures. Of their final ten shows, from *Jumbo* to *By Jupiter*, eight out of ten were highly successful, with seven smash hits coming in succession. Beyond any measure of the quantity of output, Rodgers and Hart exerted influence, individually and collectively, on the art **130** of songwriting and the musical comedy models of the period. Lorenz Hart revolutionized lyric writing; he took what was once a functional commodity for a melody and charged it with wit, imagination, and charm. Like Rodgers's gift for composing, Hart's writing seemed always spontaneous and effortlessly produced. Yet what appeared effortless to others was actually craft in action, a craft more remarkable for being one of the first in its field. In the song "Blue Room," Rodgers gave Hart a melody in which the initial measure's C-natural note is repeated in the second, third, and fourth measures of the song. Hart responded by reflecting the melodic idiosyncrasy with the triple rhyme *blue-new-two* on the repeated note while the word *room* repeats on consecutive rising tones.

In Richard Rodgers, Hart found the ideal creative complement. Rodgers fitted into Hart's will to experiment with rather than worship the old formulas. They were leaders in their field, not followers. Every show had its own idea, plan, strategy, and execution. Their only "formula" was not to have one. Within the freedom of such a relationship, Rodgers strove to translate into notes what Hart was trying to do with language. David Ewen wrote:*

> An unexpected chromaticism or modulation neatly coincided with an unusual turn of phrase or rhyming scheme; a fleet, light-hearted tune reflected perfectly the sparkle of Hart's smartness; a poignant melody would follow Hart in some of his gentler moods. The singleness of expression of words and music in every major Rodgers and Hart song is one of its salient strong points.

Rodgers and Hart carried their spirit of experimentation into the theater where both applied considerable skill to the task of eliminating all gaps between story and song. They introduced the device of rhythmic dialogue with musical accompaniment to ease transitions from scene to song. On other occasions, short musical pieces of four to sixteen measures prevented the book from stopping dead for a song. As with the Princess Theatre collaborators, Rodgers and Hart aimed for song derived from the

* From *Richard Rogers* by David Ewen (New York: Holt, Rinehart, and Winston, 1957). Used by arrangement with the author and his agents, Scott Meredith Literary Agency, Inc.

131

immediate needs of the play. Much like Oscar Hammerstein in his work with Kern and Romberg, Rodgers and Hart were guided by a vision of what American musical comedy could become. Motivated by this dream, and gifted with vigor and talent, they probed the possibilities of their materials to a degree not expected from so popular and established a team. One fundamental aspect of their enlightened adventuresomeness which underscores their fundamental respect for theater has been noted by Deems Taylor. In those days, the musical comedy score averaged eighteen numbers, including reprises. The Rodgers and Hart average for twenty-seven shows was thirteen songs each, including reprises. Taylor reasons then that an average of thirteen numbers per show allowed for fifteen more minutes of dialogue and thus permitted the story to play out with more validity and plausibility than the highly organized succession of song cues which passed for the musical comedy book of the period.

Rodgers and Hart were uncompromising in their search for new ideas, structural formats, and production methods. In *On Your Toes* they explored the role classical ballet might play in a Broadway musical by engaging George Balanchine as choreographer. *The Boys from Syracuse* adapted Shakespeare to serve the interests of the popular musical stage ten years before Cole Porter and Sam and Bella Spewack wrote *Kiss Me Kate.* The apotheosis of the Rodgers and Hart craft was *Pal Joey,* which Lehman Engel in *The American Musical Theatre* rates as the first great American musical comedy piece of the mature genre, and one of the twelve great American musical shows of all time.

Rodgers was reserved, methodical, responsible, and professional. After an interview with Rodgers, Carol Hughes offered this estimate of the man:

> He is conservative, quiet, demonstrative, with a concise attitude about living. A deeply conscientious man who has taught his heart to listen to his head, he holds a devotion for his job that is akin to religion, but he can and does discuss it in cool, undramatic fashion.

Compared to Rodgers, Hart was erratic, irresponsible, careless, and moody. Although a witty, brilliant, and gifted writer, Hart actually disliked writing unless he was in the proper mood, and his moods were as varied as they were unpredictable. Once Rodgers took great care in having Hart confined to a hotel room for the purpose of working on a show, only to have him excuse himself to go down to the lobby to buy a cigar—and not be seen for several days. When Rodgers would invite Hart to his country home, Hart would disappear for hours at a time. Only later did Rodgers's daughter Mary reveal that as a child, she would play with "Uncle Larry" by hiding him up in a tree hut. Despite the chasm that separated their personalities, habits, and extratheatrical interests, Rodgers and Hart were united by a deeply human bond. As Rodgers put it, "Our fights over words were furious, blasphemous, and frequent, but even in our hottest moments we both knew that we were arguing academically and not personally. I think I am quite safe in saying that Larry and I never had a single argument with each other."

If a deeply human concern bound man to man, a solid method of collaboration bound composer to lyricist. Usually, the melody was written first and the lyric fitted to it. Larry Hart described the process:

> If I am trying to write a melodic song hit, I let Richard Rodgers get his tune first. Then I take the most distinctive melodic phrase in his tune, and work on that. Next I try to find the meaning of that phrase and to develop a euphonic set of words to fit it.

According to Rodgers, this method was necessary to the collaboration because Hart hated work and it "took the challenge of an existing tune to rouse him to his best efforts. Usually, the finished product developed according to the traditional form of a verse or lead-in followed by a refrain of thirty-two measures. A song like "There's a Small Hotel" from *A Connecticut Yankee* reflects the customary AABA song structure: main melodic idea (eight measures), repeat (eight measures), release (eight measures), and return to main idea (eight measures). The collaborators employed structural variations when warranted. "Thou Swell" from the same show follows the ABAB pattern that allows for equal emphasis on the melodic ideas in the main motif and the release. While subject matter, locale, theme, story, and style varied with each song and show, Rodgers chose to write music whose inflections and style might suggest but never imitate his subject. As he argued in *Musical Stages:**

> Frequently, composers try to reproduce the musical sound of a specific age or locale, often with some success, but I think it's a mistake. It leaves the writer open to comparison—usually unfavorable—with the real thing, and at best only reveals re-creative, rather than creative, skill.

Rodgers and Hart grew apart gradually during the late 1930s when Hart caved in from the impulses of a deeply disturbed person. When Rodgers confronted his partner with the professional problems caused by his alcoholism and irresponsible behavior, Hart just said, "I've never really understood why you've put up with me all these years." Then Larry Hart walked out, Rodgers cried, and it was over. Larry Hart died in 1943, just months after the opening of *Oklahoma!*

Rodgers and Hammerstein

Why are Rodgers and Hammerstein so important in American musical theater? They formulated and demonstrated principles about their craft that elevated the popular musical stage from entertainment to art. Those principles follow.

First, Rodgers and Hammerstein supported the conviction that the song was the servant of the play. According to Hammerstein, "It is wrong to write first what you think is an attractive song and then wedge it into a story." Similarly, Richard Rodgers in discussing the work of his collaborator urges students of the lyricist's craft to examine Hammerstein's lyrics out of context for no other reason than "to discover their indispensability to the context itself." With a few notable exceptions, such as *Show Boat, Pal Joey,* and perhaps *Of Thee I Sing,* an unequivocal

---

* From *Musical Stages* by Richard Rodgers (New York: Random House, 1975). Reprinted with permission.

Rodgers and Hammerstein elevated the popular musical stage from entertainment to art with *Oklahoma!* (1943), the first "integrated" Broadway musical. (Photo: The Lynn Farnol Group, Inc.)

concern for "context" (the book) in musical comedy production was not common practice before *Oklahoma!* The typical pre–Rodgers and Hammerstein musical turned on a contrived plot whose only function was to provide a dramatic excuse for the sequence of hit songs assembled for the score. The songs avoided dramatic function in music and lyrics. Little more was demanded than that they be slipped neatly into the story and be charming, delightful, or lovely. When talent failed to generate suitable material, writers and composers could drag anything appropriate out of their files. As a result, book shows played like a revue. Songs, dances, and scenes could be transposed just about anywhere. Problems of dramatic context never arose because there was no dramatic context. *Oklahoma!* changed all that. Songs and dances that propel the plot, set a specific mood, reflect a situation, and depict a moment in a character's development either work to their task or travel out of the show. When Rodgers

135

and Hammerstein retained a song, you can be sure it was for a specific purpose. The score to *South Pacific* demonstrates how song can service the play. The music of the songs for Emile de Becque has a broad and powerful sweep, a continental flavor, a romantic fullness. The music *is* the character captured in sound. The music of the songs for Nellie Forbush have a lightness, bounce, and charm for the same reason.

Second, the shows of Rodgers and Hammerstein were the product of sincerity. In the light of criticism directed against them and their universe of sweetness and light, it is important to understand that Rodgers and Hammerstein believed sincerely in what they wrote. Hammerstein particularly embraced life's simple truths and considered it his duty as an artist to communicate that truth in words, characters, and situations designed to impel audiences to feel. Joseph Fields, who collaborated on the book for *Flower Drum Song*, said that "Oscar really believed that love conquers all, that virtue triumphs, that dreams do come true." Hammerstein himself never denied that he was a sentimentalist. "There's noth-

Rodgers and Hammerstein never wrote anything without hope in it. Miyoshi Umeki sings "A Hundred Million Miracles" in *Flower Drum Song*, 1958. (Photo: The Lynn Farnol Group, Inc.)

ing wrong with sentiment. . . . The things people are sentimental about are the fundamental things in life. I don't deny the ugly and the tragic—but somebody has to keep saying that life's pretty wonderful, too. Because it's true. I guess I just can't write anything without hope in it." Rodgers's response to their critics has been, "What's wrong with 'sweetness and light'? It's been around quite a while. Even a cliché, you know, has a right to be true." Consequently, they applied their philosophy of life to creative work in the theater, and advised other writers to do the same, to "mean it from the bottom of your heart, and say what is on your mind as carefully, as clearly and beautifully as you can." Getting the right words and notes on paper was a matter of expressing what is honestly felt, instead of conjuring up fancy and clever rhymes, foolish jokes, tricky titles, imitative phrases, and "boffo" fill-in materials. This preoccupation with honest, sincere sentiment was based on experience, Hammerstein's bitter and extended experience of failure. If anything, it taught him to trust in self and its honest projection. He always remembered his failures, learning as he remembered.

> I was too easily satisfied with my work. I was too often trying to emulate older and better lyric writers, saying things similar to the things they were saying. It would have been all right had I been content to imitate the forms of their songs, but the substance would have been mine and it was not.*

Third, artistic integrity allowed the collaborators to focus on the direct, the honest and the natural instead of precedent, expectation or "sure bet." Oscar Hammerstein told Lewis Funke of the *New York Times*,**

> There are no magic formulae. . . . There are no hidden charts either. Aside from trying to judge the temper of the times, we don't know what the public wants. In fact, I think it's the other way around. We decide on what we want to do and then we hope the public will want it.

---

* From Oscar Hammerstein II, *Lyrics*. Copyright © 1949 1977 by Oscar Hammerstein II. Reprinted by permission of Simon & Schuster, a Division of Gulf & Western Corporation.

** Copyright © 1949 by The New York Times Company. Reprinted by permission.

Oklahoma! remains the outstanding example of this spirit. The first act is almost over before the female chorus makes its entrance, and gorgeous girls have been the glorious privilege of musical comedy since *The Black Crook.* What could have been a serious conflict between honest dramaturgy and traditional showmanship was avoided by simply being true to an original conception, by agreeing to start the play in a manner suitable to its content. The logic in Rodgers and Hammerstein's method brought about much that is admirable in *Oklahoma!* for by refusing to acknowledge the pressures of prevailing "showmanship," they were always free to make decisions consistent with the best interests of the material.

Finally, Rodgers and Hammerstein maintained a professional union for theatrical production that involved all allied talents connected with musical comedy production. Musical theater has always been concerned with forging many arts into a coherent and satisfying whole. Rodgers and Hammerstein productions achieved a total collaboration between producer, writer, composer, director, choreographer, actor, scenery, costumes, lighting, orchestration, management, and public relations. This "new" collaboration, realized through a careful definition of roles, was born out of a deep respect for musical comedy as theater. The collaborators wrote,*

> Not much less complex than war is the musical theatre, and its complexities are compounded by the fact that the relationships among its components are not defined and absolute as they are in the army, but subtle, tenuous and usually emotional. . . . A quick glance at the theater program for any musical show reveals a staggering number of separate elements. These must complement each other and become fused if the total effort is to stand as a valid artistic representation.

During their career together, the sensitive relationship between lyric writer and composer was the model for the working methods of the Rodgers and Hammerstein army of theatrical collaborators. Just as the choice of words had to relate to the choice of notes to express a proper emotion, so too did an orchestration have to relate to plot or character elements, or costumes to choreography, or lighting to the special facial contours of an actor. The constant objective was always dramatic musical ex-

* Reprinted with permission of American Theatre Press, Inc. From *Playbill*, 2, Oct. 27, 1958, Richard Rodgers and Oscar Hammerstein II, "Words and Music: A Partnership."

pression, in which every component part amplified the other. In giving their best and expecting no less, Rodgers and Hammerstein forged new levels of performance and production that have since become the standards for musical comedy in America.

METHOD OF COLLABORATION

The Rodgers and Hammerstein method of collaboration which evolved from their work on *Oklahoma!* set the pattern for all subsequent efforts. Initially, long and elaborate planning sessions would center around the choice of material, the story line, and the probable place of the songs in the book. The creative intimacy of the collaborators would be evident from the very first move made in the project. Oscar Hammerstein wrote:*

> Dick and I stay very close together while drawing up the blueprint of a play. Before we start to put words or notes on paper we have agreed on a very definite and complete outline, and we have decided how much of the story shall be told in dialogue and how much in song. We try to use music as much as we can.

Once the initial planning had been completed, they approached the "interior" problems—the mood of a song or scene, the attitude of a character or line. This stage of invention involved the treatment of minor characters, variations in the story line, the nature and limits of the dialogue, comedy, and romance, agreement on setting, atmosphere, possible actors, and staging techniques.

Once it was mutually decreed that their idea for a show was sufficiently organized, Hammerstein would leave for his farm near Doylestown, Pennsylvania, while Rodgers would work in his New York apartment or Connecticut home. Hammerstein would pace about the room, pausing only to write his lyric down in longhand. His next step would be to polish it until he could do no more to perfect it. Only when completely satisfied would he send it to Rodgers by mail or read him the line over the telephone. Rodgers would promptly set the lyric to

* From Oscar Hammerstein II, *Lyrics.* Copyright © 1949, 1977 by Oscar Hammerstein II. Reprinted by permission of Simon & Schuster, a Division of Gulf & Western Corporation.

139

music in a comparatively short amount of time. Since Rodgers composed in his head, he was free to work anytime and under any circumstances. He has never been "grounded" to a piano. Songs have been fashioned in taxis, in offices, in bed, at lunch, at home on sheet music forms, or even on scraps of paper. The classic example of the Rodgers phenomenon was "Bali Ha'i," written in five minutes' time on the back of the page of typewritten lyrics which Hammerstein had given him while at lunch at producer Joshua Logan's apartment. Another instance involved "Happy Talk" for the same musical. Hammerstein sent the lyrics for "Happy Talk" to Rodgers's Park Avenue apartment where the composer was in bed with a cold. Concerned over the lyric's safe arrival, Hammerstein figured out the time of the probable delivery, added ten minutes, and called Rodgers. By then, the song was completed. "It's discouraging," Hammerstein once confided, "to deliver a set of lyrics to Dick and have him phone next morning and say, 'It's all done. When's the next coming?'"

Although the actual act of creating the song is swift, the creative process leading up to it is involved and time-consuming. Rodgers claims that the melody line only comes to him after much concern for the type and function of the song he is asked to create. Reacting to a similar incident with lyricist Alan Jay Lerner, Rodgers claims,

> I get no place trying to tell people that story isn't true. The song situation had probably been going around in my head for weeks. Sometimes it takes months. I don't believe that a writer does something wonderful spontaneously. I believe it's the result of years of living, of study, reading, his very personality and temperament. At one particular moment all these come together, and the artist "expresses himself."

Rodgers and Hammerstein needed a reason for writing a particular song, and that reason was usually found in a dramatic situation. In *Oklahoma!* for instance, the songs are so skillfully woven in and out of the story that it becomes almost impossible to imagine the story without them. Rodgers told a reporter, "My big involvement is with . . . people. Not the actors, but the characters they play. I must know how they feel, and then I can give **140** them a song to express it." Rodgers didn't write his tunes for the sake of fun, profit, or Tin Pan Alley, just as Hammerstein didn't write verse for its own sake. The secret of their successful collaboration may have been their mutual concern for theater. Hammerstein made clear his position on this subject when he confided, "I don't believe that either Dick or I would be very, very successful essentially as popular songwriters—writers on songs detached from plays. We can write words and music best when they are required by a situation or a characterization in a story."

The joint responsibility of composer and lyricist to the planning of a song and the story that encases it has always been a feature of the Rodgers and Hammerstein philosophy. Hammerstein has written that the musician is as much an author of the piece as the poet who produces the words. Integration was the desired state in which two crafts, their two kinds of theatrical talent, were welded into a single expression that was not so much a compromise as a unity. This was possible because Hammerstein did have definite ideas on the treatment of a score. Rodgers, on the other hand, responded immediately to words and reacted with enthusiasm to those which would suggest musical ideas to him.

Having some knowledge of the materials of each other's craft, Rodgers and Hammerstein chose to operate on an honest "veto" basis. If Hammerstein submitted a questionable lyric to Rodgers, it would be discarded. If Rodgers set an unacceptable melody to a Hammerstein lyric, it too would be eliminated. The veto power was rarely used, but on those occasions, the material was completely tossed out, never filed for future use.

THE RODGERS AND HAMMERSTEIN CONTRIBUTION

The Rodgers and Hammerstein collaboration brought about the maturation of the American musical. Before them, promise: after them, achievement. Why? Theirs was the talent, forethought, and skill to consolidate the musical theater's resources and reshape them into the splendid artifacts that became models to a generation.

Theirs was the destiny to make two miracles. They turned musical theater amusement into theatrical art and that American art into a highly profitable business. How? Deep faith—that out of the tradition would evolve a form more serious in intent and vital in its culture than any previously known theatrical phenomenon.

Specifically, Rodgers and Hammerstein set new goals for the American musical play and devoted their considerable collaborative resources to the successful realization of their aims. *Oklahoma!* was more than a spectacular critical and popular success; it was a revolutionary manifesto that banished *June-moon* musicomedy as it raised the "integrated" musical to the seat of power and influence. The concept of an "integrated musical" deserves our attention. Many twentieth-century musicals aimed for and achieved an homogenous synthesis of dramatic, theatrical, and performance components. The Princess Theatre shows, the Romberg operettas, and the best of

In the integrated musical, all the elements of a musical show push the story forward. *Carousel,* 1945. The opening sequence. (Photo: The Lynn Farnol Group, Inc.)

When the book became the prime generator of the production, song became the servant of the play. *The King and I*, 1951. (Photo: The Lynn Farnol Group, Inc.)

Rodgers and Hart held the stage on that merit. Integration implies more than synthesis, however; it implies the successfully coordinated ability of all elements of a musical show to push the story forward out of proportion to the individual weight of each element. Not only does every element fit perfectly into an integrated show, each functions dramatically to propel the book forward.

Rodgers and Hammerstein liberated the creative musical theater community from the tyranny of formula and the sure bet. When the book becomes the prime generator of a production, everything flows out of its unique and special stream. What is imposed is doomed to wash away. What is discovered in the stream should flow effortlessly with the current. That includes music. The primacy of the book dictates that the song become servant to the play. Corollary principles follow. Lyrics assume a critical role in the book and a greater balance must be achieved between drama and music.

Rodgers and Hammerstein's prescription for a serious musical theater led to a consistently distinguished **143** popular art based on a genuine affinity between honest collaborative principles and cherished American values. Not by chance was theirs an art of the people and for the people. Hammerstein stated, "The musical play today has created valid pictures of American life, made important comments, developed the art of integrating dancing, singing and dialogue to an extent never before achieved." He added, "It is a playwright's mission to tell his story so that it will be understood by a great many people, not just a negligible few." More than once did a considerable public rally to support their work in the face of critical disapproval. After all, they wrote less for the press than for the anticipated line at the box office on a winter afternoon.

Rodgers and Hammerstein set new standards for the musical theater book. They were the first consistent practitioners to regard the book as dramatic architecture. Story, plot, sentiment, and optimism surfaced regularly, but always within a framework crafted to show off each to its best advantage. The book became an all-inclusive aesthetic umbrella under which to gather in close proximity all the creative, interpretative, and administrative elements of a musical theater project. Comedy developed out of character and situation. Out went the interpolated jokes, puns, and slapstick of adolescent musical comedy; in came the most endearing humor of people in a predicament. A new standard emerged that dared the audience to take principal characters seriously. Acceptable motivation, projected psychological makeup, and down-to-earth humanity in their characters secured for the American musical its final liberation from cardboard stereotypes. At last were presented particularized people, one of a kind and memorable.

Rodgers and Hammerstein used very practical means to achieve their artistic ends. Their idealism was always tempered by their first-hand dealings with the people and problems of their trade. For instance, in *Oklahoma!* both men supervised the casting; Rodgers himself labored with the orchestra in the pit during the New Haven tryout—not to mention the special singing classes of four or five hours each which he personally held to train the cast to sing Hammerstein's lyrics "carefully and clearly."

144

Rodgers and Hammerstein believed that comedy must develop out of character and situation. Julie, Carrie, Mr. Snow, and ensemble. *Carousel,* 1945. (Photo: The Lynn Farnol Group, Inc.)

The Rodgers and Hammerstein capacity for practical doing extended beyond the artistic and into the production aspects of their enterprise. The so-called cock-eyed optimists were among the first producers of their time who fought to bring about a fair regulation of expenditures so necessary in an industry plagued by rising costs. They met frequently with the Committee of Theatrical Producers to devise methods for reorganizing elements from the entire theatrical profession into a structure with a more modest and efficient economic balance. Yet economic matters never infringed upon their responsibility toward other theatrical interests. For instance, both collaborators would participate in any serious meeting or conference affiliated with the affairs of the theater. They were always enthusiastically involved in extensive auditions for, and the solid support of, new talent. Rodgers once told Frank Aston of the *World-Telegram and Sun* that he maintained an open-door policy regarding

145

auditions "selfishly, to find new young people who will do tomorrow what Merman and Martin do today." During every season, Rodgers and Hammerstein kept themselves knowledgeable of bookings, proposed projects, and cast changes. When in production, no detail escaped their attention. The "hem of a costume" or "the flower in a vase"—nothing was too "insignificant" to command their interests.

So much has happened to America, music, and the theater since the 1940s and 1950s: accelerated pace in modern living, redefinition of roles and models in human relationships, radical change in audience mood and morality, spectacular inflation in Broadway economics, a growing chasm between the "popular song" and the "show song," and the emergence of creative artists who demonstrated alternative theories and approaches to a stageworthy musical. Yet Rodgers and Hammerstein remain in their place at the center of the mature musical theater tradition, rooted firmly like some awesome and venerated monolith in the soil of America. Rodgers and Hammerstein gave the popular musical the opportunity to be what it is and will continue to be: art that holds the stage and invites each new generation to experience, learn, enjoy, remember, imitate, parody, or reject. Otto Harbach explained to Oscar Hammerstein that the elements of a musical play are like the

> ingredients that go to make a fire—logs, kindling, matches, a good fireplace, etc. . . . All these ingredients, he said, are necessary, but they won't make a good fire unless they are properly assembled. . . . When everything works—when the logs crackle and the bark sputters, when the blue and gold flame waves and flies toward the chimney and sends out warmth and good feeling to cheer a room full of people, it is because some . . . fellow knew how to put one log on top of another in just the right way.*

Rodgers and Hammerstein knew how to assemble the elements of a musical in just the right way. It is in keeping with their spirit that now, other young and serious craftsmen appear to redirect the evolution of American musical theater into yet another unique, satisfying, and impressive form.

* Copyright © 1953 by the New York Times Company. Reprinted by permission.

STEPHEN SONDHEIM

Although the golden age of the integrated American musical lasted for two decades only, the Rodgers and Hammerstein model so raised the creative conscience of gifted theater artists that the period sustained a sequence of shows the best of which represent the most enduring work of the mature musical theater. How familiar are those shows; like friends, they seem to have been with us always. *Brigadoon. Kiss Me Kate. Guys and Dolls. My Fair Lady. West Side Story. Fiddler on the Roof.* But as the era and its creative imperatives eased into the period of cultural shock epitomized by the undisciplined excesses of *Hair,* alternative musical theater practices emerged to threaten all the fundamental values of the creative musical theater establishment. To survive, the Broadway musical would either destroy the past and construct itself in an entirely new image, or retain the tradition in a revitalized form suitable to the new sense of modern life. Stephen Sondheim committed himself to the latter course, and the road has carried him through an adventurous creative life that accounts for a first-rate body of work, the most intellectually stimulating, finely crafted, forward-looking accomplishment of the modern musical theater. No matter how you respond to it, one undisputed fact remains. This is important work, a solid body of uncompromisingly original musical theater material relentlessly true to itself and to its creator.

Oscar Hammerstein II, neighbor, friend, father-image, model, and mentor, passed on to Stephen Sondheim the same mantle of tradition that Richard Rodgers inherited impersonally from Jerome Kern. Hammerstein taught the young Sondheim how to structure a song with the beginning, middle, and end of a one-act play, the importance of every word in a lyric, the value of simple, direct expression, the primacy of content in the theater song, and the necessity for writing from the truth of what is genuinely felt or believed. Eventually, Hammerstein outlined a course of study that became the basis for Sondheim's serious preparation for a professional career. The project: write four musicals in a prescribed sequence. First, take an admired play and turn it into a musical. Second, take a bad play or one that can be improved and turn it into a musical. Third, take a nondramatic work like a novel or a short story and adapt it into a musical. Fourth, create an entirely original musical. The four apprentice musicals created by Sondheim during his college years introduced him to the creative process, the writer's craft, and prepared him early for professional creative work.

Later, Sondheim's work absorbed other major influences. From Bert Shevelove, coauthor of *A Funny Thing Happened on the Way to the Forum,* he learned never to "sacrifice smoothness for cleverness" in a field where good ideas demanded clear expression. The playwright and librettist Arthur Laurents passed on vital information about dramatic writing. Doesn't the theatrical songwriter build into a song what the dramatist builds into a scene? Songs and scenes rely on subtext, a performance energy that grows out of the dramatic principles inherent in an idea. No continuous and consistent drama happens by chance. Nor does it hit the mark by riding on the words alone. In performance, drama must surround the song as it surrounds the scene in nonlyric theater.

149

Philosophy
and Principles

Stephen Sondheim writes songs for the theater, virtuosic songs that grow from the dramatic ideas inherent in a show's concept to *become* the very drama earlier songs would only reflect. Before him, a Broadway musical evolved from stories audiences wanted to hear, of how everything turns out all right in the end and of how being human and alive is worth it all. That approach worked for Rodgers and Hammerstein because they believed in it. Sondheim doesn't. His musical theater trades the world of emotion for the world of intellect, sweetness for bite, warmth for detachment. A lesson learned from Oscar Hammerstein II: Write only what you believe. This Sondheim does, and according to the principles which follow.

The book determines the musical, its style, tone, mood and nature and placement of the songs—everything. For Sigmund Romberg, Jerome Kern, and Rodgers and Hammerstein, book meant story. For Sondheim, book means idea, the concept that makes possible the most effective mobilization of the elements of the musical into a smooth and compact theater art. The book initiates, fuels, and sustains collaboration. It determines direction, performance, choreography, design, and orchestration. A great show with a terrible book? Never. The book is the show.

The book must focus on characterization. People matter in life; people matter in art. Only when songs for the theater reveal the drama in character; the "rumblings beneath the surface," do they achieve validity in Sondheim's concept of dramatic songwriting. His songs seldom achieve popularity outside the context of their shows because the composer creates material exclusive to context, to the particular characters for whom the songs are written and the specific situation that precipitates the dramatic revelation. The songs so rely on the atmosphere of a particularized dramatic situation that they defy transplantation with the tenacity of any vital organ determined to remain in the body for which it **150** was designed. All great writing for the theater thrives on the dramatic particularization that provokes interest and sustains attention. We believe in Hamlet, Blanche Du Bois, and Nellie Forbush because they are formed of particulars that come together into a unique, whole, and special personality. Their lines belong to them alone, to their voices and their lives. Recognizing that the principles of dramatic writing apply to theater songwriting, and that drama is character, Sondheim composes by maneuvering subject, development, meter, rhyme, rhythm, melody, and harmony to reveal in song the particularized complexity of character. The people on the stage secure his total creative allegiance, not the people in the audience, the record companies, or the sheet music business. No major composer of popular musical entertainments so consistently and determinedly avoids the technique guaranteed to promote the immediate popularity of a song: the reprise. When song is drama and drama must develop, then score must be committed more to development than to repetition. Some of the best songs in his repertory are composed on the road because Sondheim values the creative stimulation of experiencing character in action on the stage and writing for them. Some attribute this creative hesitation to procrastination. Sondheim's position: you write best for what you see in performance, the character, scene, mood, tempo, feeling, atmosphere, and interpretation. "Comedy Tonight" was written in response to specific performance stimulation, as was "Being Alive," "I'm Still Here," and "Send in the Clowns." Were Stephen Sondheim in a position to underwrite and administer his creative preferences, the entire score would be written only after the cast has begun rehearsal or public previews.

Content dictates form; what the songwriter has to say determines how to say it. *Oklahoma!* opened with the uncommon scene of an old woman churning butter while a young cowboy serenaded offstage because the text generated that kind of an opening. Arthur Laurents fashioned the brief libretto for *West Side Story* on purpose and in the belief that *Romeo and Juliet* was melodrama anyway and it would be senseless to write for character when there was none. Consequently, Sondheim determined that all *Company* songs would function as comment and counterpoint because he felt that the librettist did not write characters who sing. For *A Funny Thing Happened on the Way to the Forum,* a farce of great wit, breakneck pace, measured diction, and measureless grace, Sondheim conceived a score where songs interrupt the action and that could be removed from the show without destroying the development of the plot. Realizing that such a brilliant farce would play at a breathless pace, Sondheim wrote songs as moments of welcome relief. When the label "concept musical" applies to a Sondheim show, it means this: music, lyrics, dance, direction, dialogue, and design integrate in production to support a thought. That thought dictates everything.

Lyrics

Stephen Sondheim reveals this allegiance to book, character, and concept in lyrics that issue from two fundamental assumptions. First, all lyrics exist in time. Poetry, verse, and other literary forms exist in space in that reading and enjoyment respond to the will of the reader who can linger over lines, stanzas, or pages to suit his pleasure. A song marries lyrics to the relentless tempo of the music which pushes the lyric along at speeds a listener cannot control. Poetry can be read, reread, or put aside; a theater song lyric must be grasped and understood the first time through or you risk losing the thought for the rest of the performance. In this, the writer of the theater lyrics shares many of the platform concerns of the public speaker. Criteria for effective communication are the same. There is no second chance once a statement is sounded. Sound symbols provide basic communication. Nothing escapes time, pace, rhythm. Anyone who has ever had to express coherent thoughts that respond to a rhetorical objective in the prescribed time of a speech knows the terror inherent in the territory as well as the value of clarity in diction. So does the theater lyricist, an artist who writes for characters who speak and whose dramatic life and credibility depend on effective oral communication with the audience. While simplicity insures clarity, the prospect need not condemn lyricists to simple truths, clichés, or bromides. Rather, the standard should provoke the creative mind to discover new, effective, and clear language combinations that carry the message in a way like no other. The true artist discovers what did not exist before. An example of this clarity of thought embodied in clear language patterns joined to the restless inertia of a waltz tempo occurs in the score for *Follies*. The song is called "Could I Leave You." Read the lyric. You will understand much about the characters, the situation, and the emotional current of the scene immediately.

Second, lyrics live on the sound of their music and must be underwritten. Lyrics burdened with lush images, concentrated meaning, robust rhetoric, and convoluted development war with their companion (music) already rich with the sound of melody, harmony, and rhythm. Important lyricists who understand this principle work from thoughts in language that can appear conventional on the page only to soar on the wings of song. The lyrics that begin the refrain in "Summertime" *(Porgy and Bess)*, "Oh, What a Beautiful Morning" *(Oklahoma!)*, "Maria" *(West Side Story)*, and "Do You Love Me?" *(Fiddler on the Roof)* illustrate the point. Read each lyric aloud. Then sing each lyric aloud. Notice how the lines sound ordinary, flat, and undistinguished when read. Add music and the words soar on an arc of sound that crowns them with a splendor each was incapable of achieving as verse. Now add music to overwritten lyrics and look for the opposite effect. Underwritten lyrics arise; overwritten lyrics sink, drowning like soggy, leaden cargo in a sea of sentimentality. Operetta suffered from lyrics whose catastrophic voluptuousness condemns many fine melodies from the early American musical theater to discreet orchestral background music in restaurants, waiting rooms, and elevators. Repeat the earlier procedure with songs from an operetta score. First, read the lyric aloud. Then, sing the lyric aloud. The lyric doesn't improve, does it? If the weight and texture of a lyric so affects the outcome of **153** a song, then it follows that lyrics must help shape the music as well. Since mature craftsmen in the Hammer-stein-Sondheim tradition write lyrics before or simultaneously with the music, the sound produced can follow or even *be* the sense of the lyric. Didn't Richard Rodgers create melodies often whose structural profile followed the content of the Hammerstein lyric? The spiritual anthems like "You'll Never Walk Alone" and "Climb Every Mountain" rise in an inexorable linear musical motion up the melodic scale to reflect the accumulating spiritual intensity developed in the lyric. The diction of Sondheim's lyrics shapes the music in similar fashion. The brief, vigorous, staccato syllables of the word *com-pa-ny* elicit their musical counterpart in the staccato notes that give character, development, and form to the song "Company." Phrasing and rhyme in the lyric shape music, too. Can it be chance that the rhymed "ladies in attendance" and "fire opal pendants" in "Liaisons" *(A Little Night Music)* sound on the very same musical phrase? Or that the technique is repeated in the same song on the rhymed "become of them" and "some of them"?

Corollary principles follow from Sondheim's two assumptions.

A good song in a musical must generate a type of theatrical moment that cannot be duplicated in the non-lyric theater. When music ignites the dormant power packed into a lyric's tight and rigid form, the stage should explode with character, thought, or emotion. These are the moments audiences anticipate; these are the moments audiences remember. The "Soliloquy" for Billy Bigelow *(Carousel)*. "Rose's Turn" *(Gypsy)*. The spontaneous eruption of joyful celebration for Eliza's accomplishment, "The Rain in Spain" *(My Fair Lady)*. The overwhelming final "follies" sequence *(Follies)*.

The good dramatic songwriter must build subtext into the lyric. Give the actor something to act! Give the director something to play! Drama doesn't happen by chance. Observed principles of dramatic construction create the fundamental conditions for drama. Here, dramatist and lyricist share the same concerns. Study Sondheim's lyric for "The Ladies Who Lunch" *(Company)*. Note how the lyricist provides the actress playing Joanne with the context, language, and emotional surge **154** to play out in the song the character's bitter fury of ironic self-knowledge that underlies the literal subject of the song.

A good lyric *reveals* to the audience the characters who could not have the omniscience to know or explain themselves with total accuracy. In other words, do it, don't talk about it! This is an important principle because irony can be one of the most satisfying techniques of the dramatist's craft. Dramatic motion, tension, interest, conflict, and suspense surface when the audience knows something the character does not. Where would the playwright go with *Oedipus Rex* if Oedipus knew and could explain? Songs that reveal dominate the score for *A Little Night Music.* Sondheim calls them "inner monologue songs" because characters sing their deepest, most personal thoughts to the audience but not to each other. Examine "Now," "Later," and "Soon" and contrast what is said to what is revealed. In "Now," Fredrik so explains the elaborate alternative plans for marital seduction that one gets the impression he won't do anything with his wife after all. He doesn't. In "Later," Henrik reveals that beneath the quiescence of his existence there lurks a capacity to rush headlong into life, now. He does. In "Soon," Anne promises to fulfill her conjugal obligations but suggests that she won't, at least not with husband Fredrik. Each song reveals something other than what the words explain literally; joined together, the trio become the central dramatic situation suggesting plot possibilities to the audience that none of the characters could possibly comprehend.

Good song lyrics find humor in character. People make us laugh through the lines they speak. The humor of character demands an appropriate dramatic situation; it fails out of context. Where jokes, gags, and slapstick can succeed when plucked from the book, humorous character lines do not. On this page, Joanne's line from *Company,* "She's tall enough to be your mother," generates little enthusiasm. Yet it is a funny line in the show, Sondheim's favorite, a line that works for the character only when delivered as a complaint in context. Another example: When the lawyer Fredrik extols the assets of

his virginal child-bride to his unbelieving ex-mistress Desiree in the song "You Must Meet My Wife" (*A Little Night Music*), it is character response to a dramatic situation that generates the laughs. Like many distinguished lyricists before him, Sondheim finds it useful to write comedy songs backwards. A climax, a twist, a punch line, or a joke must be set up carefully by all that goes before. The knowledgeable theater lyricist decides on the gem, then designs the proper setting to show it off to maximum advantage.

Good lyrics use rhyme to focus attention on the rhymed word and make it the most outstanding word in the pattern. A word that is not important should not be rhymed. Consider Sondheim's application of this principle in "The Little Things You Do Together" (*Company*). The dual rhyme schemes of *share-swear-wear* and *enjoy-annoy-destroy* communicate the meaning, development, and ascension of the lyric. Sondheim prefers rhymes to identities. A rhyme indicates the recurrence of corresponding vowel sounds preceded by a different consonantal sound; the vowel and consonantal sounds are the same in an identity. *Bug* rhymes with *rug*. *Delight* and *polite* are identities. Inner rhymes, rhymes that occur within the line rather than at the end of it interest him because they serve to accelerate the pace of the lyric. Since rhyme implies intelligence or education, rhyme must never be used arbitrarily. On the other hand, alliteration implies a bankrupt brain, alliteration being the repetition of an initial sound in more than one word in a sequence.

Music

Stephen Sondheim composes highly personal music to match the character and tone of his lyrics. Contemporary sense demands a contemporary sound, a sound the composer achieves through inventive meters, unusual melodic intervals, and complex, surprising harmonies. Although his music can suggest other times, places, or composers, as in the pastiche score to *Follies*, the ear **156** alerts the listener to the proposition: Sondheim writes Sondheim. This is not easy, pleasant, or popular music. It engages the ear, but seldom caresses it. While audiences accustomed to melody in the service of sentiment hold back from his more sophisticated rhythm- and harmony-dominated sounds put in the service of intellect, critics and students admire the craft. Lyrics sit properly on their musical phrase. When a lyric comes to an end, so does the music. Music and lyrics develop in the same way and climax at the same time. On a more complex level, Sondheim crafts (1) the individual song to become the specific content of a dramatic moment on stage, and (2) the entire score to reflect the concept of the show. For example, the *Follies* book plays out a concept that deals in the elements of time, memory, ghosts, shadows, and the past. To match score to book, Sondheim wrote a pastiche of songwriting types and styles from the recent past. To capture the delicate, romantic "Old World" flavor of *A Little Night Music*, Sondheim composed the score in distinctive 3/4, 3/2, 6/8, 12/8, and 9/12 meters.

The musicals of Stephen Sondheim preserve and renew the serious American musical theater. Unlike many composers who seem all too willing to overthrow anything to court public favor or connect with the latest trend, Sondheim and producer-director Harold Prince joined forces to experiment from a solid base within the established tradition they know and love. In this collaboration rests the talent, commitment, and experience to give future musicals new life and direction, the controlled reincarnation of that principle which has guided the serious American musical theater from the beginning: the complete integration of all elements of the musical show into an artistically homogenous form.

157

10

THE
BOOK

When Alan Jay Lerner wrote in the preface to *Brigadoon,* "I can tell you the book is all essential. It is the fountain from which all waters spring," he celebrated a conviction that dominates the creative philosophy of the mature American musical. The book comes first. That is a chronological fact, a philosophical imperative, and a practical principle.

Musical theater is a highly collaborative enterprise, a singular art achieved by the synthesis of other arts: dramatic literature, verse, music, design, recitation, voice, mime, and dance. If any one among the component arts of a musical show has the power to draw together the individual collaborative efforts of so many artists and shape their collective contribution into a unified and finished work, it is the book, that is, character, dialogue, form, placement of song and dance, tone, and theatrical values put at the service of story or concept. The musical book generates the theater in a musical theater. It is both the magic glue that binds all parts into a seamless form and the magic principle that unites all artists into harmonious community. The book *is* the show.

Philosophy

A good book is an outline of highly compressed dramatic development that provides a working umbrella for the songs and dances that distinguish an effective production. It is a skeletal play, the lead sheet of the entire show, the sturdy frame that defines the limits of everything that show can offer to its audience. In addition to standards of literary excellence, a good book prospers in proportion to the credible opportunities it offers music, dance, design, and performance to do on the stage what words alone are inadequate to do: to open up the show's thought or emotion in a succession of situations and build them to a satisfying resolution *through music and movement*. As the expression of idea or feeling through music is the major objective, everything in the musical book must set up and show off the songs. The superior musical book allows for a variety of musical expression in solos, duets, trios or quartets, choral ensembles, underscoring, segues, and ballet music that assumes a specific dramatic function in ballads, comedy songs, musical scenes, and production numbers. Consequently, the ear is the first to detect the basic difference between a play and a musical book. The words of a play project dramatic meaning through their own spoken sound. The words of a musical book project dramatic meaning through the extended sounds of lyrics set to music or the substitution of movement language for sounded language. An example of how an experienced librettist would go about this adaptation of play values to book values occurred when Oscar Hammerstein II transformed Lynn Riggs's play *Green Grow the Lilacs* into the book for *Oklahoma!* Buried in the play was an appealing and poetic stage direction that suggests the tone of the play which follows. Unfortunately, the play limits the dramatic function of its images to whatever mood values it can communicate to the cast or production staff. The audience will never hear it, and can only see it if indirectly reflected in design or performance. Oscar Hammerstein II realized that a lyric derived from the original source would soar when set to music. What the printed page of stage direction could suggest to a few became available to all in images of sound. Read the stage direction again in silence, then sing "Oh, What a Beautiful Mornin." Such are the transformations peculiar to the musical book.

Because it must reserve space for song, dance, and **162**

spectacle, the musical book cannot approach the dramatic weight of a play with deep characters and dense dialogue. Wise librettists don't try. Instead, the book writer pursues the simple and obvious in a stage world where everything is precisely what it seems to be. There is no time to probe situation or linger on all levels of a character's psyche. Thus, economy of expression accompanied by an essential companion, clarity, distinguish the musical book from the play. Should the audience miss the point in a play, there is a good chance the idea will be made again in another scene or by another character. Certainly, there is enough time and room in a play for reinforcement. The demands of the musical book allow the librettist no such luxury. The standard: make the point and move on. Not only do musicals move with their book, they move because of their book. No mean feat, since a musical book adapted from a play may lose one-half the volume (length) of the original material.

At the turn of the century when the term *musical comedy* was being used to distinguish native musical book show entertainments from comic opera and operetta, the musical book served only to string together the songs and dances that appealed most to the audience. The condition persisted well into the twentieth century. Jerome Kern revolutionized the philosophy of the book and implemented his theories successfully in the Princess Theatre shows, but the majority of producers, writers, and composers resisted his influence. The battle of the book became a long and frustrating struggle. The coalition of hit songs and star power proved to be formidable opponents. One battle stands out from the rest. Oscar Hammerstein II had been engaged to collaborate with Jerome Kern and Otto Harbach on a musical for Marilyn Miller called *Sunny* (1925). The collaborators accepted the challenge and with the energy of mutual artistic stimulation marched headlong into the producer's office armed with the dramatic and theatrical possibilities of the project. Management resisted; the show was to be an elaborate vehicle for the star. In desperation, the collaborators read a detailed outline of the plot. Marilyn Miller replied, "When do I do my tap dance?" Two years later, Jerome Kern and Oscar Hammerstein II wrote *Show Boat.*

Types

The modern American musical theater offers many types of book musicals, the majority of which fall into the broad descriptive classifications of musical comedy, musical play, play with music, modern operetta, and popular opera.

At one time the generic term *musical comedy* identified any form of American musical entertainment with an admixture of elements from operetta, comic opera, revue, burlesque, spectacle, and extravaganza. Today, the word *musical comedy* applies only to a book show with motivated songs and dances in which comedy dominates an altogether light and frivolous world of entertainment. The musical comedy experience leaves the impression of an evening's encounter with a well-designed entertainment machine, a modern, better-motivated descendant of the old-time formula musical of hit songs and snappy routines. Shows like *Annie Get Your Gun* or *Hello, Dolly* permit the audience to sit back, relax, and have a good time throughout. Musical comedy is to musical play what comic opera is to grand opera: the difference is not one of quality, but intent. Without eschewing entertainment values, the musical play aspires to serious art through ambitious content, universality of theme, prominent drama, character depth, bold form, and demanding production. The musical play envelops the audience while it entertains, goes deep where others remain on the surface. The way in which a lyric, music, or dance enhance the drama signals a musical play. The way in which the comedy of character in situation functions as relief to the drama signals a musical play. The weight of substance in a show signals a musical play. Paradox beleaguers the musical play. It is somber and complex, but at the same time enjoyable. The use of "Sunrise, Sunset" during the Tzeitel-Motel wedding scene of *Fiddler on the Roof* illustrates this paradox. Here is a sentimental song of graceful lyrics and pleasing melody, one that would stand out in the score of any musical comedy. What distinguishes the song in its musical play is context, universal sentiment **164**

The musical play aspires to serious art through ambitious content, universality of theme, and prominent drama. The death scene from *The King and I,* 1951. (Photo: The Lynn Farnol Group, Inc.)

particularized in the specific dramatic situation of the pogrom. How the musical play uses a song adds the layers of dramatic intensity that give dignity to the theatrical moment. This song in its deft context goes deep into audience emotion, finds the human spirit and caresses it. We are made to feel deeply, even cry. Yet we are grateful. On some deep and satisfying level, we have been engaged.

The play with music is similar to the musical play in temperament but not in concept. The difference between them involves critical judgment. Do lyrics, music, and dance account for the unique life of the material on stage or can the play stand alone without them? The play with music avoids making fundamental, illuminating use of the peculiar components of a musical theater. *1776* offers lyrics, song, and movement. To remove them would do little damage to the text.

Like its ancestors, the modern operetta surrenders to romance with customary charm and grace. *A Little Night Music* is not that far removed from *The Merry Widow* or *Die Fledermaus. The Fantasticks, The Sound* **165** *of Music,* and *A Little Night Music* live in operetta territory. The manner in which characters are made to act, think, and feel betrays an unmistakeable origin. Still, the writing stops short of complete escapist surrender to romance and sentiment. A new and modern chord sounds in character, plot, lyrics, and dialogue. As the opening of any musical sets the tone of the piece while it clues the audience on the nature of the evening's entertainment, we need only to turn to the "Quintet" which opens and waltzes periodically through the book of *A Little Night Music*. This is the stuff of Old World indiscretion, a lyric about an antique scandal set to 3/4 time, and ripe with the images of operetta: a remembered idyll floating on images of villages, an inn, walks in the park, gingham, and *The Bartered Bride*. Stephen Sondheim, that most book-oriented of all contemporary lyricists, repeats the word *remember* eighteen times in the lyric. Obviously, the past will be made present in this material. However, nothing old-fashioned happens in the book. The virgin wife elopes with her stepson, her husband returns to his old mistress, and the lover of the mistress returns to his wife. Nothing like that ever happened in *Naughty Marietta*. The modern operetta looks back and forward at the same time.

On the other hand, popular operas like *Porgy and Bess* and *Jesus Christ Superstar* resort to the old conventions of opera form. Everything is set to music. Consequently, the book in popular opera must be music-oriented throughout. While the style of music for popular opera varies according to period or popular taste, the conventions of the book remain fixed, so much so that comparison between nineteenth-century Italian opera and twentieth-century rock opera reveals striking similarities in quality, character, and temperament. "Summertime" *(Porgy and Bess)* has been a standard in the American popular song repertory for over four decades. To experience the song in performance on stage, however, is to become less conscious of its pop tune status than of its deep allegiance to the tradition of the lyric aria adapted to modern purpose. The tradition: an extended dramatic song with definite form and music of wide vocal compass, expressiveness, and intensity. The adaptation: vernacular lyrics. In no way did the modern shift to rock **166** music upset the continuity of the tradition. "Hosanna" *(Jesus Christ Superstar)* sounds and plays on the stage like a grand opera triumphal march written in the style of Prokofiev, while "I Only Want to Say (Gethsemane)" spins out a lyric melody in the characteristic manner of a lyric Puccini aria.

Elements

Five major dramatic elements combine within the musical book to account for its unique values, weight, and proportions. They are character, plot, situation, dialogue, and theme. The elements of a musical book are like the anatomical parts of the human body. While size, shape, and mass vary with individuals, all contribute mutually to the finished and healthy form. As individuals emphasize one body feature over another to accommodate necessity, vanity, or challenge, so does each book place unique emphasis on certain dramatic elements at the expense of others. Weight and emphasis can vary, but the musical theater philosophy which regulates each does not. The elements of a musical book must be conceived and executed for the exclusive purpose of communication in a theater through music.

CHARACTER

Character is the soul of drama. Other elements of a musical show can stimulate, excite, involve, or structure, but ultimately it is the people we remember. Nellie Forbush. Tevye. Henry Higgins. Anna getting to know the children, the king getting to know Anna—each cuts into the heart and mind deep enough to be stored in memory for as long as the show and its songs shall live. A very benign human conceit accounts for the importance of effective characterization in the musical book. When a writer creates a successful character, one who is one-of-a-kind and fleshed out in the nuances of a living being, that character becomes in action some part of us. We

167

recognize. We understand. We identify. We care. Only then are we moved to laugh and cry. When we celebrate character in the theater, we celebrate ourselves. While all writers for the stage aim for rich and full characterization, the librettists enter the race burdened with a formidable handicap: the space and time limitations of the musical book. To compensate, writers must (1) introduce simple characters immediately who are (2) recognizable to the audience as principals, (3) for whom conflicts will develop and (4) who make the audience care enough to anticipate a satisfying resolution. Remember *Carousel* and *Fiddler on the Roof?* Not only does each book illustrate the four points of the librettist's procedure, but each crafts its handiwork with the unique tools of a musical theater. *Carousel* opens with a waltz prelude set in an amusement park where we meet Billy Bigelow and Julie Jordan (points 1 and 2) and witness the jealous behavior of Mrs. Mullin (point 3) and the gradual, mounting attraction of Billy and Julie (point 4). The entire scene plays in pantomimic action synchronized to music. "Tradition" *(Fiddler on the Roof)* works in the same way, only it adds lyrics, song, dialogue, and dance.

Simple musical exposition of simple characters in simple situations need not condemn characterization to one-dimensional stereotypes. Simple characters in a musical book can be full and memorable because they have the richness of music, song, and dance to make them alive in performance. Nellie Forbush and Tevye are not complicated people. Their librettists knew enough not to throw curves about their identity, hide dark secrets, or follow hidden agendas. Their librettists knew that simple but unique characterization suffices in a theater rich in the added overlays of continuous sound and movement. The simplicity standard does not mean that characters cannot grow. What it does mean is that characters do not change, they do not become other than what we first perceive them to be. Nellie and Tevye develop throughout, but they do not change.

PLOT

Without a program for action, the well-rounded, highly motivated characters of the modern musical theater **168** would suffocate under a bell jar of undramatic immobility. To avoid this, the musical book turns to plot—a sequence of actions designed to bring out the drama in character, idea, or situation. Plot does not mean story. Plot implies a specific chart of events; story implies the tale that is told. The musical book for *Gypsy* by Arthur Laurents and *Gypsy: A Memoir* by Gypsy Rose Lee tell the same story. However, each advances a different plot. This is not as trivial a distinction as it may seem. Recent experiments with the "concept musical" where all the elements of a musical show are made to embody an idea have questioned the need for story altogether. *Company* challenged the old tyranny of story line by doing with the linear story line what cubist painting does with space. The effect can be difficult on an audience accustomed to drama as story. Where plot demands a sequence of events, *Company* offers a structure of fragments that defies the linear dramatic movement implied by a sequence of actions. However, those writers who recognize the need for plot obey a fundamental principle: the plot must reveal the drama, not tell about it. All credible drama springs from the make-believe of impersonation fueled less by dramatic narrative than by the dramatic imitation of action. Musical drama, rooted in the tradition of romantic theater, thrives on action. The romantic hero is never static. The vital, energetic activities of song and dance cannot thrive sandwiched in between a plot that cannot move the show along. What is more, characters reveal dramatic growth through what they do. All dramatic claims fail as theater when not supported by dramatic behavior. Oscar Hammerstein II knew this and embodied the principle of dramatic revelation in the finale of both *South Pacific* and *The King and I*. In each case, character in action reveals the drama in a way that encapsulates that most difficult of essential musical theater messages, "I love you." Each works because plot *shows* what a lesser librettist might be tempted to *say*.

SITUATION

Situation operates within plot as any moment that generates drama, sustains audience attention, and begs for a final resolution. Like microcosmic dramatic units, many

Situation operates within plot as any moment that generates drama, sustains audience attention, and begs for a final resolution. The finale of *Flower Drum Song*, 1958. (Photo: The Lynn Farnol Group, Inc.)

situations add up a macrocosmic plot. In addition, each must be responsive to song and dance expression. Although the majority of important musicals since *Oklahoma!* were adapted from fully realized plays, not all plays will sustain the metamorphosis into a workable musical book. Why? Certain situations resist musical treatment. The ability to recognize these situations marks the minimum professional requirement for the librettist. To be able to accumulate these situations, melt one into another, and build each unit into a complete package is what the craft of musical book writing is about. *Romeo and Juliet* has had a long history of successful adaptations in opera, ballet, and musical play because the sequence of melodramatic situations eliminates the need for words and encourages the substitution of sound and movement. Study the musical program for *West Side Story*. Except for the moment of comic respite offered by "Gee, Officer Krupke," every musical number in the score arises out of the three main dramatic situations in the book: Jets-Sharks, Tony-Maria, Anita-Maria. The progression of **170** those situations as reflected in each song tells you all you need to know about the premise, development, and resolution of that show.

DIALOGUE

Dialogue is talk, the fourth essential element of the musical book. Characters speak with each other, about each other, and, in a manner appropriate to the presentational conventions of the musical theater, to the audience. Unlike the spoken drama, the dialogue of the musical book must accept the companion language of the lyric. Where the playwright in the nonlyric theater uses dialogue to open up character and expand dramatic effect, the writer of the musical book condenses the volume of dialogue to set up the takeover of the lyric. In the mature musical theater, the song is the purpose of the scene. If the librettist fails consistently to make the song the focus of the scene, then there is no purpose in making a musical from that material. Where songs succeed as the scene, dialogue must be subject to economy of expression. Since there is less of it in the musical book, dialogue must be sharp, crisp, and to the point. Each sentence must justify its space and count for more than its literal weight in thought or feeling. Clarity must be attendant to the working librettist. Despite the attractive distractions of action, underscoring, or spectacle, audience understanding must be simultaneous with actor delivery. No better example of economy and clarity exists in the modern musical book than the critical scene in *Fiddler on the Roof* where Fyedka connects with Chava in Motel's tailor shop (Act I, Scene 8). In less than a page of dialogue, librettist Joseph Stein (1) makes two people fall in love and (2) sets in motion the mechanics for the plot's denouement. Appropriate diction concerns the professional librettist. Language must be appropriate always to character, mood, and the desired tone of the show. Read the book for *Oklahoma!* The sound, the images, and the dialect suggest the Indian Territory of Oklahoma just after the turn of the century. Read the book for *Company*. The sound, images, and usage suggest 1970 New York City. In addition, the appropriate diction of the dialogue must blend naturally into the diction of the lyrics. Read "The Surrey with the Fringe on Top" sequence from Act I of *Oklahoma!* Check the scene against the score. Note how effectively Oscar Hammerstein sails his characters from dialogue to lyric to dialogue with no break in rhythm, tone, or continuity.

THEME

To say that a musical supports a theme is not to say that a musical supports a concept. The theme of a musical show is its main idea; the concept of a musical production is how that idea is embodied or interpreted. Writers build the theme of a show into content where character, plot, and dialogue project it to the audience. Concept reaches beyond theme into some statement or image of what the show means to be, or what it intends to do, or how it will go about doing it. You may interpret the theme of *Cabaret* as: The response of the young to life's injustices must be to live a full and pleasure-seeking life. The concept of *Cabaret?* To render the theme's dramatic hedonism in the robust and decadent world of 1930s Berlin cafe life. On an elementary level, theme is to creation what concept is to interpretation. On the sophisticated level of the concept musical, concept is to creation as concept is to interpretation. Usually, concept enriches theme and gives the director and designers a handle on how to proceed. When theme dominates, however, no one quality can be more responsible for a show's universal appeal.

Attributes

No rigid rules exist for writers who must address the specific task of mixing specific ingredients into the sweet confection that is a musical show. However, the model of those works of aspiration and achievement in the active repertory of the popular American musical theater suggests that a good musical book combines the qualities **172** of romance, emotion, lyricism, and comedy. Song and dance prosper in the service of romantic love, that idealized love whose images of affection, attachment, and devotion we celebrate in art and pursue in personal dreams. Unlike the sexual love of temporary relief through biological release, romantic love promotes total involvement, the most eternal, metaphysical, and transcendental human emotion and our most vital and mutually shared human experience. Sexual love promotes repetition; romantic love promotes growth and development. One motivates the body to relatively short-lived feats of physical expression, the other incites mind and spirit to timeless poetic expression. The preoccupation with romantic love accounts for the emotional scope unveiled by our most successful musicals. Romantic love can embrace children *(Fiddler on the Roof)*, dance *(A Chorus Line)*, and noble ideals *(Man of La Mancha)* as well as husband, wife, or lover. Romantic love knows no barriers in the universe, including age and race *(South Pacific)*, class *(My Fair Lady)*, or death *(Carousel)*.

Since romantic love represents the highest aspiration of human feeling, and human feeling becomes most visible in the musical book clothed in general emotionalized attitudes, most successful musicals pursue romance through sentiment. Musical theater is romantic popular theater, a theater of all the people. Where reason eludes the mob, strong emotion does not. A playwright of the nonlyric theater can avoid broad sentiment at will; a librettist committed to musical collaboration might find the emotional power in music too powerful a force to ignore completely. It is true that the Stephen Sondheim collaborations avoid equating sentiment with love, but it is also true that the shows have never been popular in proportion to the talent and craft involved. However, the majority of smash-hit musicals in the classic musical theater repertory feature the wisely crafted, romantic-sentimental book that gives the audience an opportunity to share universal feeling, to laugh and sigh and cry together. They scramble the shared emotions of the audience, then resettle them. If the audience smiles deeply as it leaves the theater, it smiles less out of relief than

out of recognition of a shared humanity experienced in

a collective act of involuntary emotional response. The romantic-sentimental book tells the audience: you *feel,* therefore you *are*—and it is good.

Romance and feeling cannot be realized in the musical book without the accompanying quality of lyricism, that sense of the suitability of individual dramatic material for treatment in music. What latent pulse beats deep in a play, short story, screenplay, or autobiography that signals the potential for lyric theater? Precedent argues that one asset of the material would be the capacity to express emotional content rather than external characteristics or events. Certain mines, rich and deep in ore, yield to the knowing prospector a wealth of precious metal that begs to be extracted and molded into artifacts of beauty and power. The vein of gold in the mine of musical theater must be rapturous feeling. Rapture soars in the theater when it rides on the wings of music. When musical rapture soars in the service of romantic ideals and generous artistry, it is likely to consume. Great musical theater must envelop its audience. Should it fail, it is likely that the nature of the material proved unsuitable to it.

Comedy is the attribute of a musical book suitable to it always. The popular musical theater embraces the vision of life as it should be, the life filled with song, dance, and laughter. Only the truly defeated never laugh, and where in the repertory of the successful musical book do you find truly defeated characters? Comedy is a vision of life more than it is laughter. Laughter follows the acceptance of that vision because the vision of comedy makes that laughter possible. What is that vision? Simply this: everything will turn out all right in the end.

Comedy has always been the hallmark of the popular American musical theater. Comedy entertained, relaxed the audience, and gave it deep pleasure. What distinguishes the comedy of the mature musical book from its adolescent predecessors is its new nature and function in the musical book. Comedy originated outside the book in early musical comedy. Performers hired specifically for that purpose interpolated jokes, gags, or slapstick to generate the laughs. The laughter-provoking devices were general enough to be assigned to anyone in the cast and often topical enough to permit casual improvisa- **174**

The most effective comedy develops from the elements of the musical book, particularly character and situation. Ali Hakim and Ado Annie. *Oklahoma!* 1943. (Photo: The Lynn Farnol Group, Inc.)

tion during performance. In sum, comedy was cosmetic. Today's most effective comedy grows organically from the elements of the musical book, particularly character and situation. If the comedy of the mature musical book fails to amuse out of context, it is because the comedy is the context. Neil Simon can make us laugh loud, hard, and often, but do we respond to the line or to the character? Usually, the line. Joseph Stein makes us laugh in *Fiddler on the Roof,* but is it the line or Tevye we remember? The vision of comedy in the mature musical book grows from and graces its characters, and character is the soul of a dramatic musical theater. In addition, the comedy of character-in-situation provides a natural contrast in mood to the more serious moments of the book without upsetting audience belief in either. Where com-

175

edy in the past would fragment the show into moments of comedy, separate and exclusive from similarly contrived moments of romance or spectacle, mature musical theater comedy binds all elements into rich and full dramatic world. Here, comedy can relieve the mounting drama of the serious musical play and still not intrude on audience credibility. It can function in believable contrast to the pressure and tension as it sets up subsequent scenes for moments of even greater dramatic strength. Not by chance did librettist Dale Wasserman maneuver the comedy song "A Little Gossip" into position between moments of Don Quixote's dying and Don Quixote's death. Here, comedy eases the mounting gloom of the former moment as it sets up the audience for the incisive drama of the latter.

Mechanics

The musical book is a splendid engine that pulls all the elements of a musical show to a desired destination. Like any machine, it is subject to principles of dynamics which guide proper construction, explain effective operation, and calculate maximum efficiency. Brevity, particularization, tempo, and subplot constitute the unique mechanics of the musical book.

The nature of the musical book demands the surrender of spoken dialogue to the forces of song and dance. Song extends the sound of human speech in time. Song holds vowels, enjoys pauses, and repeats entire passages in the refrain. The additional time consumed by movement, dance, and spectacle deducted from the two- to two-and-one-half-hour limit on the modern musical reduces the room for dialogue to one-third or one-half the length of an average play. Compare *Pygmalion* to *My Fair Lady, Green Grow the Lilacs* to *Oklahoma!*, or *Romeo and Juliet* to *West Side Story*. The mechanical problem is this: how do you invent a rich, dramatic stage world peopled with round characters comparable in credibility with the nonlyric theater with less time and fewer **176** tools? Few librettists know the answer. The majority of playwrights never care to know. The librettist's profession is the most difficult and undersubscribed activity in the modern musical theater.

Where skill aids the writer in the pursuit of brevity, talent aids the writer in the quest for effective particularization. A musical drama commands the attention of an audience only to the extent that the writer endows the elements of the book with special and individualized characteristics. "One-of-a-kind" proves noteworthy in the world of created things. On the other hand, who cares deeply for an abstraction? For example, the book for *Company* surrounds its hero Robert with five couples, his married friends. To particularize each character, lyricist Stephen Sondheim has each call Robert by a different nickname. The opening number "Company" introduces the total population of Robert's married friends through the individual language they use to address him. Some examples: "Robby," "Rob-o," "Bobby baby," "Bobby bubi."

Time and space tyrannize the musical book. As brevity accommodates the problem of space, tempo accommodates the problems of time. The mechanics of the effective musical in performance demand that the adjective *brisk* modify tempo. The modern musical moves. With this in mind, the professional book writer builds into each scene devices that thrust the show forward into the next stage of development. Note how Joseph Stein moves *Fiddler on the Roof* forward. Its pace waits for no one. After "Tradition," all the pieces of the dramatic puzzle are on the table waiting to be moved. The librettist thrusts the audience immediately into the Tzeitel-Motel relationship. Before that affair peaks, the audience is already into the Hodel-Perchik affair that blends in similar fashion into the Chava-Fyedka relationship and the finale. Although performance accounts for the pace that audiences recognize immediately, it is the writer who controls a show's base tempo through the concept, relationship, and sequence of scenes. When a song dominates or ends a scene, the burden of tempo rests with the lyricist. In that case, lyrics of anticipation, prefiguration, or foreshad-

owing function to thrust the book forward, much as

"Something's Coming" *(West Side Story)* thrusts the dramatic action into the next scene where the dialogue for Maria parallels the earlier lyric's anticipation, so thrusting the book forward into the following scene of boy-meets-girl at the dance in the gym.

Of all the mechanics of the musical book, none is more peculiar to the musical theater than subplot, that complete, secondary, and subordinate plot that runs in counterpoint to the main plot. Since the brevity standard demands that even the most robust and ambitious book resemble a skeletal play, writers use subplot to add weight and substance to the skeleton. Subplot works for the librettist the way counterpoint works for the composer. Each fleshes out its material without an appreciable addition of time and space. Its people are like complete and independent melodies that when added to others with skill and understanding flesh out a more full and satisfying product. Why? Subplot serves the interest of *contrast*. Operetta established the first consistent use of subplot to contrast the romantic principals with the subordinate comic pair, a tradition we recognize in such mature musicals as *Oklahoma!, Carousel, Brigadoon,* and *Guys and Dolls.* Subplot serves a practical function, too; it provides the singing and dancing principals with a much-needed rest during performance.

Structure

The structure of the musical book refers to the unique organization of all the elements of a musical according to the demands of theme or concept. One principle dominates all musical book structure: content dictates form. Each idea for a musical carries with it distinctive values and possibilities that dictate an appropriate shape. That recognized, the librettist can resort to corollary principles whose consistent appearance in the best musical books merits enough critical recognition to be organized under the heading "the structural characteristics of the musical book." The first characteristic draws on the pattern of exposition, conflict, and resolution. The writer of the mu- **178** sical book can (1) introduce the principal characters and other vital elements in the opening scene or song; (2) establish the conflict that generates dramatic tension; and (3) cultivate in the audience a sincere desire for a resolution to the problem. The second structural characteristic applies to three critical moments in the sequence of a musical show: the opening, the end of Act I, and the finale. Today, the opening of a skillfully crafted musical show showers the audience with all the dramatic and theatrical elements peculiar to that production: character, situation, theme, dialogue, setting, style, tone, approach, and performance values. Since the opening is what the audience sees first, their liking it can allow the production to ride undisturbed for at least another thirty minutes. When the book demands the two-act division, the conclusion of Act I must embrace some technique to bring the audience back into the show with the interest and enthusiasm aroused by the opening. Under these circumstances, some dramatic expression of tension that prolongs the anticipation of resolution works best. This is the principle behind the dream ballet in *Oklahoma!,*

When the book demands the two-act division, the conclusion of Act I must embrace some technique to bring the audience back into the show. The dream ballet. *Oklahoma!* 1943. (Photo: The Lynn Farnol Group, Inc.)

the rumble in *West Side Story*, the pogrom at Tzeitel's wedding in *Fiddler on the Roof*. Since the Act I finale generates anticipation for resolution, it follows that Act II be shorter and less complicated than Act I. Usually, not more than forty-five minutes stands between the conclusion of the intermission and the Act II finale. Consequently, experienced writers limit the amount of new material added to Act II. New material takes time to develop, time that can serve better the crucial push toward the Act II finale. Some writers pad Act II with abbreviated reprises of Act I material. This device adds interest, requires no further development, and provides no obstacle to the show's growing momentum toward a destined conclusion. The musical theater finale should be more than a predictable resolution. It should sum up the special experience of the show. Here, the writer must send the audience out of the theater with a moment to remember, a moment consistent with the book, yet exciting by itself. Remember the final image of Tevye beckoning the fiddler to follow? The top hat and tails finale to *A Chorus Line?* "Rose's Turn" from *Gypsy?*

The era of the primacy of the musical book marks a recent phenomenon in the long history of the popular American musical theater. Even in today's enlightened creative atmosphere, the artistic potential of the book remains undeveloped. Why? Is writing a play better than writing a musical book? More satisfying? More literary? While many playwrights continue to adopt a condescending attitude when producers propose a musical project, those who accept the challenge do so with unprecedented insight and dedication. If the primacy of the musical book secured the maturity of the American musical theater, then only further experimentation and development in that area will sustain it.

11

LYRICS

The sheet music for "Blooming Lize," the hit song from the 1902 production of *The Chaperons,* printed the following credits: music by Ben M. Jerome, words by Matt C. Woodward. Forty-seven years later, the sheet music for "Some Enchanted Evening" issued a differently worded credit: music by Richard Rodgers, lyrics by Oscar Hammerstein II. What contributes to the difference between *words by* and *lyrics by* is the subject of this chapter.

The Lyric
as Literature

A theater lyric is a compact pattern of words that when set to music communicates information vital to the dramatic life of a show. Like all writing, lyrics put language to the task of expressing thoughts and emotions through the denotative and connotative meanings of words, patterns of literary development, and form.

Words signify something. Like swift and miraculous messengers, they carry to us impressions, messages, abstract ideas—in fact, anything that is possible to know. Words carry a *denotative* meaning, an explicit factual definition found in the dictionary, and a *connotative* meaning, a more emotional meaning derived from personal experience and associated less with fact than with   182 memory and imagination. Denotation marks out boundaries and specific limitations; connotation conveys association and overtones. Craft layers both in a successful lyric.

In order to elaborate and expand the denotative and connotative possibilities of language, lyricists employ such patterns of literary development as description, exposition, narration, and persuasion. To describe means to picture verbally, to develop an account in words of how things appear. Description involves the careful re-creation of the impression of experience on the senses—what it looked like, how it felt. Models of good descriptive writing abound in prose fiction. Preferences: James Agee bringing back the scents and sounds of childhood in "Knoxville: Summer, 1915"; Saul Bellow's detailed observation of the chaotic and dangerous streets of New York in *Mr. Sammler's Planet.* Theater lyrics thrive on description because only the explicit particularizes an experience for the audience. Successful description allows a community of strangers to see something together ("Kansas City" from *Oklahoma!*) or feel something together ("At the Ballet" from *A Chorus Line*). All drama requires exposition, the setting forth of necessary information concerning who people are or what has happened before. Exposition begins the motion of the plot, pushes it forward, and records its denouement. It defines the situation, reports an event, evaluates an experience. Lyricists find expository development most appropriate to presentational theater where characters confront the audience directly. "Tradition" *(Fiddler on the Roof)* demonstrates expository development in a prologue that sets up theme, character, setting, situation, mood, tone, and style. Everything that is in the show grows from the seeds planted in that opening. As in most writing, narration follows exposition. The narrative patterns of literary development respond to the question: "What happened?" It relates a connected sequence of events that tell us what happened to whom, when, where, and how. Unlike description or exposition, narration relates movement in time and that which connects the events in motion. Effective narration embraces the sequence of beginning, middle, and end. When a writer selects events and orders them properly, the lyric moves the show that much

183

nearer the desired resolution. A charming example of a narrative lyric with plot function appears in "A Trip to the Library" *(She Loves Me)*. Lyricists are drawn to the appeals of argument and persuasion as well. How often must a character in a dramatic context exploit the situation in order to convince another to accept an idea. Such is the rhetorical device that supports the lyric for Tevye's "The Dream" *(Fiddler on the Roof)*, "Many A New Day *(Oklahoma!)*, and "Something Wonderful" *(The King and I)*.

Like all writing, lyrics betray an allegiance to forms that characterize external design and identify internal structural composition. While each lyric in the mature musical responds to the principle that content dictates form, most lyrics show a tendency to the form characteristics of brevity, compactness, and periodic construction. The collaborative nature of musical theater demands that lyrics share stage time with dialogue, dance, scenery changes, and instrumental music. Consequently, most theater lyrics operate within a framework of 80 to 120 words. In addition, those words must be compact, that is, dense with word and meaning. Density of language brings with it a most welcome asset: dramatic power. As crowded molecules of thought and feeling rub against each other in close confinement, the heat and friction generates the energy for an explosion of human expression quite unlike any other in the theater. Study a performance of "The Ladies Who Lunch" *(Company)* and notice how the lean, compact, and boxlike form of the lyric gives the performer the raw power to explode the character of Joanne across to the audience. Brevity and compactness are prizes not easily won. They represent the essential criteria for professional lyric writing that bedevil many and elude most. The challenge of the form: do more with less and make every word count. In addition, grammatical forms within the outward structure of a lyric tend to be periodic rather than loose. A periodic construction is one that leaves the completion of its main idea to the end of the unit. A loose construction does not end with the completion of its main idea, but continues with one or more modifiers. Periodic forms tend to make the point and move on; loose forms tend to tolerate **184** surplus words the wise lyricist cannot agree to support. While brevity, compactness, selectivity, and periodic construction impose rigid restrictions of the lyric writing craft, most lyricists welcome rather than condemn the phenomenon. Restrictions in art can prompt the talented to great displays of imagination, as with the ceiling of the Sistine Chapel, the fugue form, and the sonnet. To succeed, the professional lyricist must navigate carefully between the Scylla and Charybdis of freedom and restriction. Only then will the lyricist be prepared to meet the next challenge, to integrate the lyric within the parent form, the book. As form follows function, and function varies with each musical show, lyric forms must so adapt to the distinctive external attributes of the book as to appear to be natural, spontaneous outgrowths of the text.

Song lyrics differ from all other forms of literature because lyric form and musical form control each other. Lyrics offer patterns of meaning sounded through the medium of music. Words give to music as the music gives to words. In a song, the capsule containing meaning, development, and form travels through the medium of the sounds which force lyrics to exist in time as well as space. We can read a novel, short story, or lyric poem at any speed, pause at will, and reread when necessary. The reader controls time. In a song, time controls the singer and the listener. Time signature determines the speed of the song, melodic profile determines pause, and the composer determines repetition. The writing of lyrics is not so much an independent craft as an allied craft, one that is far too undersubscribed in the modern musical theater. Perhaps Richard Rodgers was right when he observed that "writing lyrics is more demanding than writing music."

Types

When Mrs. Oscar Hammerstein II was asked to comment on Jerome Kern's "Ol' Man River," she replied that Jerome Kern wrote the notes to the song but Oscar Hammerstein II wrote "Ol' Man River." The answer does more than reflect a woman's pride in her husband's work; it underscores the important but underrated contribution the lyricist makes to the mature musical theater. While tunes matter most to many in the audience, it is the idea of the lyric within the idea of the show that sustains the musical drama. Consequently, the duty of the lyricist must be to contribute the sound dramatic ideas that advance the theatrical interests of a show through the types of songs we call ballad, charm song, comedy song, musical scene, "I am" song, "I want" song, and special material.

Love is an indispensable commodity in the romantic musical theater. Most *ballads* are love songs. Therefore, all lyricists must confront the how-to-write-a-love-song problem, especially the task of particularizing that old and much abused sentiment in a fresh and appealing way. In other words, how do you say, "I love you" without saying, "I love you" and still get the message across in a manner appropriate to the material? Since most professional collaborators in the mature musical theater believe the song to be the servant of the play, their ballad ideas sprout from seeds gathered from the dramatic elements of the book. Romantic love in the theater does not happen convincingly as an inevitable attraction of two disembodied spirits. Individuals fall in love, and somewhere in each personality or situation rests singular material for the expression of that love. For instance, pride endangers the affair between Curly and Laurey for five of the six scenes in *Oklahoma!* From those people in that situation, Oscar Hammerstein II drew a lyric in "People Will Say We're in Love" that absolves the lovers from any clear and direct protestation of what each knows to be true. The lyric is a model of subtext. The truth of the message lies buried deep within the literal message of the lines, giving each performer something to play apart from the game advanced by the meaning of their lines. What an ingenious solution to the problem. The characters communicate "I love you" through seemingly ambiguous commands that begin with the word "don't." Since the music of an effective ballad can easily overpower the emotions, the lyric of the ballad must be underwritten. If not, a rising melodic curve with lush attendant harmonies could **186**

The charm song offers a moment of warmth and
well-being in a world where everything turns out
well in the end. Miyoshi Umeki singing "Flower
Drum Song" from *Flower Drum Song*, 1958.
(Photo: The Lynn Farnol Group, Inc.)

very easily sink the song in a dangerous sea of sentimentality. The lyrics of most operetta ballads illustrate the
principle. Their pseudopoetic words saturated with the
rapturous expression of nineteenth-century romantic sentiment and set to lush, European melodies strain the dramatic credibility of even the most adoring of audiences.
To model a lyric on them means disaster, for they provoke
audience response directly opposite to what is intended.

A theater that markets well-being as well as romance
needs the *charm song*, an intermediary lyric of optimistic
content that calls for equal emphasis on lyric and music.
To charm means to please and delight. The charm of
musical comedy is that it pleases with a vision of a world
where everything turns out well in the end. In this context, charm songs encapsulate those moments of warmth,
187 satisfaction, and well-being that must necessarily popu-

late the world of musical comedy. Audiences love a charm song. They respond with a smile and a sigh, knowing they can sit back, relax, and enjoy. The best charm songs exploit dramatic situation, particularly those intervals of temporary relief where appealing characters celebrate the positive values in life. Great art can be said to be moral in that it sustains life by contributing to the affirmation of what is right and good in the human experience. The charm song builds on that belief by extending those life-affirming dramatic moments through the medium of music. Rodgers and Hammerstein never denied the optimistic content of their work for the theater. In fact, they sought out opportunities in each musical to frame their positive world view in a charm song conceived as a direct message to the audience delivered by a character in a teaching experience, like Anna instructing the children of the King in "Getting to Know You" *(The King and I)*, Bloody Mary advising Liat, Cable, and us to "Happy Talk" *(South Pacific)*, and Maria reminding the Mother Abbess of "My Favorite Things" *(The Sound of Music)*.

Since the popular musical theater requires comedy, the lyricist must come up with fresh, imaginative, and funny song ideas that he can develop in a way that provokes laughter from the audience. The precedent of successful *comedy songs* argues for a laughter that flows from our observation of another person's problem, embarrassment, calamity, or pain. The comedy song in a dramatic framework turns the frustrations of life into laughter. It brings a sudden relaxation of tension, a deep pleasure and welcome delight. This it cannot do if the comedy lyric begs audience sympathy. The audience must feel the pain and experience the deflation of human pretense in a benign way. Playacting is a false situation, and that makes the pain and suffering endurable. The most endurable comedy lyrics follow this prescription: Put a sincere and likeable character in a difficult situation, create an incident that warrants a complaint, and set up a payoff conclusion in rhythm and rhyme. The formula applies to both the short-joke and the long-joke comedy song. A short-joke comedy lyric demands a series of payoff jokes in ascending order of effectiveness; a long-joke comedy lyric demands an extended setup that pays off in the sin- **188** gle punchline that ends the song. Keeping in mind the demands that a short-joke comedy song makes on the lyricist, turn to "Bewitched" *(Pal Joey)* and "Respectability" *(Destry Rides Again)* for evidence of how Larry Hart and Harold Rome put character and situation to the task of assisting craft in making an audience laugh outright. Alan Jay Lerner turns a similar trick with the long-joke comedy song with "My Mother's Wedding Day" *(Brigadoon)*.

The *musical scene* is more ambitious than the comedy song lyric. Here, the lyricist must devise a package of language that allows an entire dramatic action to be set to music. Such a scene can be any unit of development within the musical book. An ambitious example of the musical scene? Act I, Scene 8, *West Side Story*, where Tony, Maria, Anita, Riff and the Jets, and Bernardo and the Sharks anticipate the coming of night in the ensemble reprise of "Tonight." This example reveals much about the nature and function of the musical scene. Note that the entire scene is revealed in the language and forms of a lyric, and that it still functions to take the plot from the serene and lyrical scene in the bridal shop (Act I, Scene 7) to the violence and anguish of the rumble (Act I, Scene 9). The advantage of setting it to music? The composer can extend the developing force and tension in harmonies and rhythms that carry the audience into a total experience of the content in the sound, language, and movement that is peculiar to the musical theater. In the musical setting, solo voices give way to duet, then trio, then quartet, and climax in the passionate quintet for principals and chorus.

Dramatic Function

Musical theater lyrics give substance to moments of concentrated thought and emotion set up by the book and suggested by the music. Each lyric turns thought into statement, intent into action, and feeling into expression in order to reflect character, propel plot, embody theme, contribute to mood, set tone, define setting, or act as relief.

Lyrics reflect character through diction, grammar, and rhetorical patterns. An audience must assume that the words a character is given to sing reflect something about that character. The language in the art of the song cannot be as spontaneous or haphazard as it is in life. What we speak and how we speak sets us apart; that is the premise behind what is made to happen in *My Fair Lady*. Compare the vocabulary and grammar of Henry Higgins in the song "Why Can't the English?" to the lyricist's choice of words for Eliza Doolittle in the immediately following song, "Wouldn't It Be Loverly?" Henry Higgins sings a correct, multisyllabic English filled with urbane allusions and clever observations. Eliza sings on

Theater lyrics differentiate characters through diction, grammar, and rhetorical patterns. Julie Andrews and Rex Harrison: *My Fair Lady*, 1956. (Photo: Theatre and Music Collection, Museum of the City of New York)

simple words, inaccurate spellings, and faulty modifiers. Their grammar separates them, too, as do the rhetorical devices each is made to employ in lyric expression. Stephen Sondheim used rhetoric for character contrast in *Company*, Act I, Scene 6. He devised a calm, clear, and concise construction for the rational Paul to play against the frantic, run-on constructions for crazy Amy.

A lyric propels plot when song language translates thought into action. One of the assumptions that underwrites the "I want" song lyric is that the character expresses desire in order to do something about it. A simple test can determine whether a lyric functions in the service of plot. Measure the progress in the life of a musical show from before the lyric to after the lyric. That distance equals plot development. For example, prior to "Something Wonderful" *(The King and I)*, Anna refuses to see the King. After the song, she agrees to go to him. Another example. "The Dream" *(Fiddler on the Roof)* carries Tzeitel from the butcher to the tailor. Note that in each case, the song lyric works like a scene to spur on the plot to a new stage of development.

Lyrics embody theme. Any show that pretends to develop a story or advance a concept cannot afford to absent its main idea from musical treatment. From 1943 to 1959, Rodgers and Hammerstein fashioned nine musical plays around themes of love and hope. At least one song lyric in each show embodied the optimism that both felt to be an essential ingredient in their work:

Oklahoma!	"Oh, What a Beautiful Morning"
Carousel	"June Is Bustin' Out All Over"
Allegro	"One Foot, Other Foot"
South Pacific	"A Cockeyed Optimist"
The King and I	"Hello, Young Lovers"
Me and Juliet	"A Very Special Day"
Pipe Dream	"Sweet Thursday"
Flower Drum Song	"A Hundred Million Miracles"
The Sound of Music	"My Favorite Things"

Songs of theme or concept must appear as the opening number in the score if their idea is to be of any theatrical use to the production. One legacy bequeathed by director-choreographer Jerome Robbins to the American musical theater is that the lyricist must tell the audience immediately what the play is about. That principle accounted directly for "Comedy Tonight" (*A Funny Thing Happened on the Way to the Forum*) and "Tradition" (*Fiddler on the Roof*), and indirectly for "Company" (*Company*).

Lyrics contribute to mood. Words can induce, sustain, or reverse a state of mind. Built into language are qualities derived from their sound and connotative associations that create their own atmosphere in the darkness of the theater. Whisper the following words aloud, and hear their echo rush the mind into a far and peculiar state. *Brigadoon. Bilbao. Bali Ha'i.* The best lyricists know that sound must echo sense, and the idea for a lyric goes far to color the mood of the song's theatrical moment. Specific ideas draw images, phrases, and rhymes from the lyricists' imagination that channel an aura as well as a meaning to the audience. From a base in the literal, the professional lyricist generates the waves of associations that carry an audience into the desired state of mind.

Lyrics set the tone of a show, particularly when diction and phrasing embody a style. Despite extravagant differences in locale, the nine musical plays of Rodgers and Hammerstein never varied in their sweet, sentimental tone. On the other hand, Stephen Sondheim's lyrics contribute much to the extravagant differences in tone established in each of his scores.

Lyrics define setting, and that means time ("Oh, What a Beautiful Morning") and place ("Oklahoma!") as well as social and psychological environment ("Lonely Room" from *Oklahoma!*).

However, not all musicals employ lyrics to integrate, intensify, propel, or project the elements of a musical drama. Some scores prescribe songs that exist for their own sake. The musicals of Kurt Weill and Bertolt Brecht personify the alternative to the integrated musical theater philosophy of Rodgers and Hammerstein. Since Brecht theorized much about devices in the theater for breaking illusion and keeping emotion in check through interrupting devices, it was natural for him to insist on wonderful, haunting, and idiosyncratic songs that interrupted the book.

Stephen Sondheim adapted the principle purposefully in *A Funny Thing Happened on the Way to the* **192**

Forum, where each song functions as a necessary pause to the relentless pace of the farce, and in *Company*, where the songs argue with or comment on character and action.

Techniques of the Lyricist

Theater lyrics are compact units of communication that submit well to a beginning-middle-and-end system of organization. The beginning of a lyric engages audience attention and announces the subject or title. The middle develops the main idea according to writer's purpose. The end of the lyric provides the resolution, the final word, the point beyond which the lyric could no longer develop. When a lyric develops in such a linear and cumulative fashion, we identify the development by the term *lyric ascension*. Read the lyric of "Some Enchanted Evening." Note the lyrical ascension as the idea ascends from the speculative "You may see a stranger" to the emphatic "Never let her go." Contrast the idea of each A section within the AABA lyric format. The lyric ascends from what you may see, to what you may hear, to what you must do when you find your true love. Each section builds on its predecessor to intensify the experience of increasingly involved romantic action. As ideas ascend in "Some Enchanted Evening," so can words and phrases ascend within a line or stanza. Watch meaning intensify within just one stanza of Ira Gershwin's "They Can't Take That Away from Me," as the lyric ascends from the mundane idea of holding a table knife, to the romantic idea of dancing until three, to the undisputably important idea of changing a life. For comic effect, the lyricist can ascend away from the sublime instead of toward it. Cole Porter achieved just that effect in a stanza from "You're the Top" *(Anything Goes)*, where the lyric idea "descends" from a Shakespeare sonnet to Mickey Mouse. The restrictions of vocabulary need not limit the scope of lyrical ascension. Porter's title for the song "It's De-Lovely"

193

(Red, Hot and Blue) descends into neologism, that is, an entirely new word.

The professional lyricist employs patterns of metaphorical language as well as patterns of organization and development. Effective imagery tied to the sound of appropriate music can evoke an imaginative context far richer and more affecting than anything made possible by the more literal statement of dialogue alone. Nature imagery brings to *Oklahoma!* what show business imagery brings to *Gypsy:* the atmosphere, mood, and tone of the subject embodied in the musical language that reveals each world to the audience.

As sensory suggestion supports metaphorical language, intellectual implication supports allusion. Theater lyricists employ direct or implied references to add dramatic dimensions to a character, situation, or event. All particularized characters speak from a frame of reference peculiar to them alone. Singular characterization draws from the who, what, where, when, and how that is never the same for any two individuals. Stephen Sondheim's choice of *caftans, brunch, wealth, optical art, Life magazine, Pinter,* and *Mahler* implicate the character Joanne ("The Ladies Who Lunch," *Company*) in personal, social, and aesthetic patterns of behavior unlike those of any other character in the cast. Specific allusions make "The Ladies Who Lunch" Joanne's song. It is her statement in her context and could not be performed credibly by another character or interpolated out of the score and into another show.

Mechanics

The theater lyric is a compact engine of communication designed to carry a dramatic load a specific theatrical distance. Like any other machine, the theater lyric is subject to properties and principles of operation peculiar to it. These principles constitute the mechanics of the lyric and are grouped under the headings of form, meter, rhyme, and vocabulary.

Since the songwriting craft involves blending language and music into a song, lyric form must be compatible with music form. The following pattern outlines the most traditional lyric form in the modern musical theater:

VERSE (Secondary Importance)
A Statement of "lead-in" or "set-up" of main idea
B Development or extension of Verse A

REFRAIN (Primary Importance)
A Statement of main idea or title
A Development of main idea
B Contrasting thought or idea that sets up final A
A Resolution or ultimate ascension of the main idea

Lyrics like "Can't Help Lovin' dat Man" *(Show Boat),* "Younger than Springtime"*(South Pacific),* and "Tonight" *(West Side Story)* adhere to this prototype. Fortunately, the AABA models adapt well to variations. A lyricist can choose to forgo the verse altogether with no adverse dramatic or musical consequences, as in "Some Enchanted Evening." Most often, variations occur in the refrain. The standard AABA form adapts to ABAB and ABAC and any other minor variation that responds to the needs of the musical book.

Form controls the shape of the entire lyric; meter reflects the pattern of stress in the syllables within each line. When lyricists speak of the ability of a lyric to shape the musical phrase, they refer to the meter inherent in any combination of words that must figure into any final determination of the musical setting. Consequently, lyricists draw on the equation: stress in meter equals accent in music. The English language submits to four degrees of stress that can be measured in units of two or three syllables called *feet.* The first and most common of these is the iambic foot, a metrical foot of two syllables, the first unstressed and the other stressed. The word *forgo* has two syllables, the first unstressed and the other stressed. Using the symbols / for stress and 0 for no stress, we can illustrate the iambic foot as 0 /. The trochaic foot reverses the stress pattern of the iambic foot. The first syllable is stressed, the second is not. The word *token* and the symbol / 0 illustrate the trochaic foot. The anapestic foot consists of two unstressed syllables followed by a stressed one, as illustrated in the phrase *ill at ease* and the symbol 0 0 /. The dactylic foot measures meter of three syllables, the first stressed and the following two unstressed, as in the word *happening* and the symbol / 0 0. Patterns of stress in the metrical foot concern the songwriter who strives for a natural-sounding marriage between words and music. Departures from the standard result in awkward musical settings. "The Surrey with the Fringe on Top" represents a successful model of music accents that conform to the metrical units in the lyric. The book demands that composer and lyricist respond to situation by creating a theatrical image of the horse-drawn pleasure carriage. The result:

CLIP-clop–	*CLIP-clop–*	*CLIP-clop* (image)
	yields	
(/–0)	(/–0)	(/–0) (trochaic foot)
	becomes	
Chicks and	*ducks and*	*geese . . .* (lyric)

None of the mechanics of a lyric strike the senses with more impact than rhyme. *Wood's New World Unabridged Rhyming Dictionary* defines rhyme as "the repetition of an identical accented vowel sound, as well as all the consonantal and vowel sounds following; with a difference in the consonantal sounds immediately preceding this accented vowel sound." In other words, rhyme involves two elements: the repeated accented vowel sound and the different preceding consonantal sound. *May* rhymes with *day*. Each word repeats the accented vowel sound *a* with different preceding consonantal sounds *m* and *d*. Spelling differences in the vowel sound do not affect the rhyme. The word *june* rhymes with the word *moon*. *U* and *oo* produce the same vowel sound despite a difference in spelling. Lyricists deal extensively in rhyme because rhyme puts great emphasis on the word rhymed, while a good rhyme gives a line freshness and punch in presumably just the right place. Since rhyme invites attention, lyricists use it to climax a thought, bring focus to a message, or set up the punchline of a joke. Rhyme helps the audience to hear, understand, and remember words. The use of rhyme sets up patterns of audience expectation. Once an audience perceives a **196** rhyme scheme, it can expect only rhymed words in certain places, words that can be guessed at if not heard clearly in the theater. Prose dialogue sets up no such expectations. When words are lost, they are lost without a clue to their sound or sense. However, lyricists must be careful in the use of rhyme because rhyme implies intellect and education in character. When the lyricist chooses to rhyme, the end rhyme (a rhyme that appears at the end of a line) becomes the most obvious type employed. Oscar Hammerstein II used end rhyme in "You've Got to Be Taught" *(South Pacific)* to focus attention on three words that make the point of the song: *afraid, made,* and *shade.* It is a technique he employed much earlier to end the "Soliloquy" for Billy Bigelow that climaxes Act I of *Carousel,* where the rhyme scheme focuses attention on the words *buy, try,* and *die.* Each word is critical to the character and the drama. The word *buy* explains the character's motivation, *try* describes the action forthcoming, and *die* foreshadows the climax of the plot.

In addition, lyricists use rhymes within the lines known as inner or internal rhymes. They tighten up construction, speed up delivery, and enliven the song's performance. Effective inner rhymes appeared in American musical theater as early as 1925 when Lorenz Hart engaged the ear and brain simultaneously in the virtuosic "Manhattan" *(The Garrick Gaieties)* where the *Manhattan-Staten, Coney-baloney,* and *Yonkers-conquers* rhymes greet each other before each line ends. Identical rhymes require less imagination but are used by serious lyricists nonetheless. An identical rhyme occurs when the writer chooses to repeat the same word at the rhymed intervals in a lyric pattern, as in the refrain of "Younger than Springtime" *(South Pacific).* Composite or mosaic rhymes feature two or more single words in rhymed pairs. To achieve a composite rhyme, it is necessary that the opening consonantal sounds be different and that the accent vowel in each word correspond. Composite rhymes can be internal rhymes. Stephen Sondheim set the composite internal rhyme *style a-Delilah* in "Beautiful Girls" *(Follies).* Imperfect rhymes or near-rhymes appear most often in pop or rock lyrics but rarely in the theater lyrics of serious writers. Why? Imperfect rhymes are not true rhymes. The word *foul* does not rhyme with *soul.* To force this imperfect rhyme is to miss the target, skirt the objective, and discredit the craft.

Lyricists who value rhyme use the technique in patterns known as the rhyme schemes. Do not confuse rhyme scheme with the lyric form. Lyric forms like AABA or ABAC describe the total structure of a lyric. A rhyme scheme like a-b-a-b or a-a-b-b describes the specific agreement of end rhymes within lyric form. Thus, the rhyme scheme a-b-a-b represents a four-line sequence where the first and third lines end in one rhyme while the second and fourth line end in another. Other options are available, like a rhyme scheme that calls for but one rhyme, as in a-b-c-b. Here, the first and third lines do not end in a rhyme but the second and fourth lines do. Ambitious lyricists can use different rhyme schemes within a single refrain to contrast the A statement with the B statement in the AABA lyric form. Alan Jay Lerner used the device for "There But for You Go I" *(Brigadoon):*

REFRAIN

$$
A\begin{cases}a\\a\\b\\b\end{cases}
\quad
A\begin{cases}a\\a\\b\\b\end{cases}
\quad
B\begin{cases}a\\b\\a\\b\end{cases}
\quad
A\begin{cases}a\\a\\b\\b\end{cases}
$$

While every lyric employs language according to dramatic need or theatrical purpose, general vocabulary considerations prevail. A critical study of an anthology of great theater lyrics like Lehman Engel's *Their Words Are Music* confirms the simple, brief, and clear nature of theater lyric language. All musicals play out in time. Time that is lost can never be recaptured. Simple and direct language helps the lyricist avoid costly misunderstandings. Furthermore, the American musical theater evolved into a popular form of entertainment, a form of the common people for whom an elitist vocabulary would be inappropriate. The popular vocabulary need not be simpleminded. Simple tools in the hands of the talented fashion great art. Thus, the principal language objective for the professional lyricist becomes this: find fresh, new ways to use the active working vocabulary. **198**

Sources
for Lyric Ideas

Picture yourself writing the lyrics for a musical adaptation of a successful play. You have agreed with your collaborators on concept and the placement of the songs. You retire to your study. Poised over paper and pen in hand, you pause. A thought occurs. You reject it. Too trite. Another pause. You break the uncomfortable spell with an unnecessary chore, perhaps sharpening a sharp pencil, rearranging the desk, boiling water for unwanted tea. You return to the desk. Sit. Wait. Nothing. Where does the lyricist begin? Experienced professionals suggest (1) the book, (2) the book writer, (3) the composer, (4) other collaborators, and (5) personal experiences that can be related to the material. The elements of the book generate most sound lyric ideas. A specific character, plot, theme, situation, dialogue, or setting may suggest an idea appropriate for lyrical expansion. Should that fail, take Stephen Sondheim's advice and consult the book writer. Book and lyrics explore the same dramatic territory, encounter similar obstacles, and benefit mutually from effective theatrical solutions to shared problems. The composer can be a major resource, as can be the director, choreographer, and designers. Finally, trust related personal experiences. They can be metamorphosed into dramatically valuable ideas. The creative mind works by association. Our senses gather the little moments of sensation we store unconsciously in the mind's library. Like all library materials, each lives to be used.

Criteria for
an Effective Lyric

If great writing issues from what a writer knows and believes, then great lyrics issue from craftsmen who have the honesty and confidence to believe what they write. Oscar Hammerstein summed up this standard in "Notes," from *Lyrics:**

> The most important ingredient of a good song is sincerity. Let the song be yours and yours alone. However important, however trivial, believe it. Mean it from the bottom of your heart, and say what is on your mind as carefully, as clearly, as beautifully as you can.

If sincerity describes the ideal attitude, then universality describes ideal content. A truly popular theater must deal in truths and values common to audiences everywhere. The most effective lyrics are those which particularize in expressions appropriate to the book the universal thoughts and sentiments all men recognize. Only then do songs forge bonds of identity between theatrical experience and audience memory, between language sounded by the lyric and emotion remembered, between actor in performance and an audience of strangers. The standard for an effective lyric in the modern musical theater hides in the paradoxical expression "particularized universality." A lyricist who deals exclusively in universals is likely to write in generalities too broad and ordinary to command attention. A lyricist who particularizes excessively is apt to produce material too personal or obscure for successful communication.

Since song lyrics live as sound, lyricists observe elementary phonetic principles. High notes register best on open vowels. Sing the words *far, go,* or *love* on a high note. The sound carries. Now sing the words *day, tree,* or *sky.* The closed vowels restrict the larynx and inhibit full voice projection. Lyricists mind their consonants, too. The hard consonants *t* and *k* should be avoided. Try to sound the consonants as you sing the words *street* or *walk* on a high or sustained note. The accurate sound of the word fails to carry. Since effective theater songs must end with the performance punch that pulls applause, last lines in lyrics attuned to phonetic principles do much

* From Oscar Hammerstein II, *Lyrics.* Copyright © 1949, 1977 by Oscar Hammerstein II. Reprinted by permission of Simon & Schuster, a Division of Gulf & Western Corporation.

to bring the song home and draw out audience appreciation.

Finally, effective lyrics for the theater must give the performer something to act. Therefore, the majority of important musical theater lyrics intensify or extend the drama in the book. These lyrics of subtext establish continuity between dialogue and song, forging one unbroken sequence of drama for performers to act out before an audience. The song *is* the scene in the musical theater. If the playwright gives the actor something to act, so must the lyricist.

The craft of the theater lyricist developed more rapidly and extensively than any other in the fertile soil and hothouse atmosphere of the twentieth-century American musical theater. Nourished by the talent and dedication of its artists, theater lyrics moved from promise *(Show Boat)* to fulfillment *(Oklahoma!)* to innovation *(Company)*. Within that brief evolutionary cycle, "words by" metamorphosed into "lyrics by," and that phenomenon does a great deal to explain much of the accomplishment of the modern musical.

12

THE SCORE

If you believe that music makes the musical, then answer the following questions. What can music do in the theater? How does it go about doing it? Is there really such a thing as a theater song? What are the attributes of an effective score? If specific answers elude you, read on. The music of musical theater demands more than casual appreciation.

Function

Music cannot state meanings, explain characteristics, determine natures, or prescribe limits. Nevertheless, composers harness all its expressive energy when they adapt music's power of *suggestion* to the dramatic elements of the musical book. In the theater, music *is* what music does, and what it does it does through aural connotation. Accept that premise, and a series of principles emerge that outline the function of music in the theater.

First. Music can reinforce the emotion in drama in a way that cannot be duplicated by language alone. Music defies the time standards of spoken language. The vocalist who holds a note or extends a phrase works within a convention where sound has more time to take liberties with a syllable, word, phrase, or sentence. Read the lyric of a ballad. Now sing it. Notice how the addition of music extends the experience of the sounded idea. This phenomenon is not just a matter of taking longer to perform; it points to the tremendous opportunity music gives the composer to extend dramatic expressiveness. For example. The actor can say, "I love you" in just so many ways, all of them short. Time limits his interpretative possibilities. The composer, however, gives the singer more time to interpret the message. Cole Porter takes seven beats to set the three words in "I Love You," while Richard Rodgers gives the principals in *Carousel* eight beats plus a ritardando. Techniques like the ritardando characterize music's unique potential for emotional expression. In music, ritardando indicates a direction to the performer to become gradually slower. The tempo of spoken language allows for no such conventions—at least, none that would be acceptable to the general public. In addition, music reinforces emotion through the sound commentary afforded by simple chord accompaniment. The speaking voice offers its own melody. If anything, accompaniment to that voice distracts the listener. On the other hand, accompaniment complements musical expression. Harmonious chords add an overlay of sound and support to a musical statement; dissonant chords add an overlay of tension and conflict.

Second. Music can be employed to reinforce dramatic action. Drama demands movement; so does music. Theirs is an allied destiny. Music in the theater can initiate, heighten, and reinforce movement that plays unadorned before an audience in the nonlyric theater. That is why in the mature musical theater a score must be more than a collection of hit tunes or soothing melodies. The serious score that succeeds becomes a musical metaphor for the show. What happens in the score happens on the stage. Each musical number in *West Side Story* makes a strong aural statement about what's going on. Consider the Prologue. The book calls for plenty of action. Jets move on a Shark, Sharks move on a Jet, Jets and Sharks move on each other. Study the score. Note how Leonard Bernstein makes music of comparable, supportive action. The time signature moves from 6/8 to 2/4 to 6/8. Anxious rests and violent musical accents abound. The movement and the music are one.

Third. Music can establish and maintain a tone ap- 204

propriate to the dramatic atmosphere of a work. Where diction alone accounts for the tone in a play, diction *and* musical styles account for tone in a musical. One reason the serious composer for the musical theater avoids drawing on completed compositions from his files to supplement a score is that where character and situation may be interchangeable, the tone of the entire piece is not. Think of how accurately Leonard Bernstein's Overture to *Candide* sets the tone of the musical and how impossible it would be to adapt that style, character, and spirit to any mature musical in the standard repertory.

Fourth. Music can personify, prefigure, and predict, particularly when the composer resorts to the operatic technique known as *leitmotif,* a short musical statement made to represent a character, event, or emotion. Consult your favorite Wagner or Verdi score for ample illustration of the effect and the procedures designed to achieve it. Remember, music is a language that communicates meaning through association. When set to lyrics, music can provide connotative support for the denotative meaning of the words. In this sense, the vocabulary of a musical theater embraces symbols that are fuller, richer, and more expansive than the vocabulary of the spoken drama.

Fifth. Music can set and sustain a dramatic mood. The musical theater book favors characters, situations, and themes that make an audience feel. When mood is a particular state of feeling, as it is often in the musical theater, music can be used to induce, maintain, direct, dissolve, change, or terminate the emotional atmosphere created by the elements of the musical book. Sometimes rhythm creates mood. The actor moves in rhythm, gestures in rhythm, speaks in rhythm. Rhythms vary within and between scenes. Watch for the variations in the intensity, color, and focus of the lighting. Music in the theater makes mood aural as well as visual. Sound colors the atmosphere on stage as surely as do hues and tints.

Sixth. Music can function as an acceptable transition device between the parts of a musical show. Where the nonlyric theater resorts to the visual punctuation of dim-out, blackout, or curtain to suggest a change of scene, the musical theater can bridge one scene with another

without interrupting the flow of the show, as in the orchestral figure known as the *segue*. The composer can use music in the theater to connect one section of the show to another the way a writer uses connectives or linking expressions to insure coherency in a composition.

Finally. Music generates dance. A theater of spoken language limits movement and spectacle to pomp, ceremony, or group conflict. Without music to transport the body into steps, combinations, and patterns, the actor must work from the limited kinesthetic palette of acceptable posture, movement, and gesture. The music of a musical theater opens up the body of the performer to an expressive potential being explored still in the most recent works of director-choreographers.

Components

To harness the enormous energy of music and channel it into theatrical expression, composers control the use of its principal components: melody, harmony, and rhythm.

A *melody* is a movement of musical tones capable of great expression—in other words, a sequence of sounds whose arrangement pleases the listener. Fortunately, musical procedures exist that allow the composer to make a dramatic statement through melody comparable to the particularized statement of the lyricist. Unlike the composers in the adolescence of the American musical who wrote hit songs for immediate enjoyment, modern composers for the serious musical theater seek to embody dramatic objectives in the melodies they create. Richard Rodgers knew that the repetition of a single tone in a melody is apt to produce sounds with a sleepy, hypnotic effect. It is not by chance, then, that the melody for "The Surrey with the Fringe on Top" reveals the dramatic content of its scene. This is more than just a charming, appropriate song. The music encapsulates the situation and gives the leading players something to act. It works in the theater because the melody represents an aural image of the lyric. The melody suggests in sound what the lyrics say in words. What melodies can suggest varies with melodic pattern and application. For instance, a melody formed by step movement from one tone to the next suggests a flowing or gliding quality. So constructed, the first five measures of "Out of My Dreams" *(Oklahoma!)* reinforce with music the image of a young girl gliding out of a conscious state into a dream of love. On the other hand, leaping motion in a melody projects a dynamic and vigorous state, as in "My Favorite Things" *(The Sound of Music)*. Often, composers make the range of a melody communicate dramatic values. A melody of narrow compass suggests a sedate or moderate manner, whereas melody with a wide range allows for the more open expression of freedom and excitement. Secure the score to *The Sound of Music.* Contrast "An Ordinary Couple" with "Climb Every Mountain." Note how the range peculiarities in each melodic profile serve lyric content, character, and dramatic function. Furthermore, the composer can resort to melodic intervals to suggest dramatic values. When the distance between one note and another is one-half step, the *minor second* interval is apt to generate a feeling of intensity or excitement. Other intervals like the perfect fifth which begins the refrain to "People Will Say We're in Love" *(Oklahoma!)* register the musical equivalent for the resolute commands each character endures from the other. The composer understood these characters, appreciated their situation, and responded to their lyric with perfect fifth intervals that ride each command: "Don't throw . . . ," "Don't please . . . ," "Don't laugh . . . ," and "Don't sigh. . . ."

Since dramatic scenes are like musical compositions—both value patterns of alternating strong and weak beats—composers can use *rhythm* to contrast the dramatic values in different situations, to dramatize character in music, and provide the momentum for dance. The *West Side Story* book trades on the extremes of dramatic situation: war and peace, love and hate, estrangement and reconciliation. The drama in the "Prologue" and "The Rumble" grows from tension, hostility, conflict, and violence. As mentioned earlier, the rhythm in both compositions jumps from 6/8 to 2/4 to 6/8 as if to hold up an aural mirror to the action of each scene. When romance prevails during "Maria" and the "Balcony Scene," the composer sets each scene apart musically from the others with a slower, more expansive 4/4 rhythm. Rhythm performs a similar function in the "Oh, What a Beautiful Morning" opening of *Oklahoma!* What did the book bring to Richard Rodgers? A radiant summer morning and a boy and girl in love. How did Rodgers respond to that setting and situation? With a radiant waltz in 3/4 time.

Composers can use rhythm to compare and contrast characters. In *The King and I,* Anna communicates much about herself in two early numbers, "I Whistle a Happy Tune" and "Hello, Young Lovers," set to an appropriately sedate 4/4 and a smooth, languid 6/8 rhythm. In direct contrast, Richard Rodgers sets the King's song, "A Puzzlement," to a vigorous 2/4 rhythm to project the dynamic energy of the robust and willful monarch. Yet when Anna becomes violently emotional in reaction to the condescending attitudes of the King in "Shall I Tell You What I Think of You," her time signature duplicates his, 2/4.

Theater composers use rhythm to compare or contrast characters. Gertrude Lawrence and Yul Brynner in *The King and I,* 1951. (Photo: The Lynn Farnol Group, Inc.)

Here, Rodgers allowed characters to trade rhythms in order to demonstrate their relationship in music. Rhythms separate characters, too. Stephen Sondheim employed the technique when he made Amy stand out from the choir in "Getting Married Today" *(Company)*. Rhythm serves musical drama well because time signatures signal the rhythms of moments in life lived at alternate speeds.

Rhythm generates the force and momentum for the regularly accented movement of the body known as dance. It parcels time into units that regulate a dancing body in space. We march to 2/4, polka to a fast 2/4, waltz and minuet to 3/4, and fox-trot to 4/4.

Musical rhythm is to visual movement what musical harmony is to visual color. The tones in a musical chord paint dramatic pictures in sound. Each harmonic accompaniment figure carries a different sound value that when tied to a theater lyric applies sound to a particular task on stage. For instance, dissonant harmonies imply nothing specific other than a discordant combination of sounds. When set to the song of the King, "A Puzzlement" *(The King and I)*, the dissonance becomes the character's state of mind made alive in sound for the audience to hear. The conflict of sounds in the dissonance is the conflict of ideas in the King. In addition, harmony can serve drama through the manner in which a chord is sounded. Jerome Kern employed the principle when he set the melody of "Ol' Man River" to arpeggios. In the theater, those arpeggios become an aural image of the timeless flow of the Mississippi River that serves as setting and symbol in the book of *Show Boat*.

The importance and versatility of music for the theater led its composers to frame a more specialized concept of the musical score. Today, the words *musical score* imply more than the sum total of musical numbers written or assembled for a particular show. A score must be a highly specialized arrangement of many fundamental types of theater songs at once unified in style and dedicated to dramatic or theatrical purpose. A serious musical theater score (1) develops from the book or concept, (2) avoids imposition and interpolation, (3) makes no concessions to the commercial market. Much to the surprise and chagrin of many in the audience, the musical score need not be popular to be effective. The most important and enduring shows in the American musical theater suggest this definition: The score is the book told in music.

Elements

Two broad classifications will govern this introductory approach to the elements of a musical score. The first includes those elements grouped according to strongly musical characteristics, like the overture, opening number, establishing number, patter songs, rhythm songs, chorus numbers, musical scene, underscoring, segue, and reprise. The second group includes types of songs according to the dramatic function implied in the lyric idea, these being the ballad, charm song, comedy song, "I am" song, "I want" song, and special material. The categories are not mutually exclusive.

The *overture* is a musical composition of varying form, length, content, and method of presentation which introduces the musical show. Orchestrators form the majority of overtures by fusing together contrasting tunes assembled from the more notable songs in the score. Usually, a vivid melodic or rhythmic motif begins the composition. Then, melodies or other musical fragments of contrasting tempo or dynamics alternate to form the body of the work. Finally, all sound resources converge in a full and rousing finale. Formula? Certainly. Listen to the overture to *Gypsy*. Its formula construction makes it no less exciting. Orchestrators who wish to depart from the formula overture find many alternatives open to them. The composer can substitute a complete and independent composition, avoid the orchestra altogether and substitute a vocal chorus, add vocal chorus to orchestra, or avoid the overture altogether. However, overture responds to valid theatrical objectives. The overture captures the attention of the audience and helps secure audience favor. *Gypsy* composer Jule Styne agrees: "All I know is that when the trumpet player started playing **210** that strip music, the audience went crazy. We were a hit even before the curtain went up." The overture puts the audience in the desired mood. An audience is a convention of strangers unprepared for active emotional participation in a theatrical experience. An effective overture can tune that audience into the same psychological wavelength of the opening scene and set up their collective consciousness for the events to follow. The overture entertains the audience. Repetition secures recognition and enjoyment. The tunes an audience carries out of the theater are those which serve triple duty in overture, performance, and reprise. The overture can suggest setting, period, atmosphere, or style, so giving the audience a foundation for recognition and appreciation of a show's initial communicative thrust. For instance, the fifth chord embellished by a grace note that begins the *Brigadoon* overture communicates the setting, Scotland, before the audience sees a single set or costume. The staccato notes and graceful musical phrases of the *My Fair Lady* overture convey the bright, airy, and refined temperament of the entire work. The dissonant chords in the opening musical statement of the "Carousel Waltz" mirror the soon-to-be-visual atmosphere of tension that underlies the principal situation in the show.

In the adolescence of the American musical theater, the *opening number* brought on the beautiful girls. Today, the opening number will more likely introduce the principal characters, describe their relationships, establish time and place, embody theme, project situation, and fix the performance style of the entire production. While all opening numbers establish, not all establishing numbers open a show. The *establishing number* asserts in music some vital idea from which the musical show can evolve. Most songs in an enduring score establish something new and beyond that of the previous song. This coordinated and cumulative movement signals musical-dramatic development within a serious musical show. However, not all theatrical situations require an establishing number. Then, the composer can add a *throwaway song* to the score, a song with no other function than to mask a complex scenery or costume change, accompany an entrance or exit, or generally divert the audience during an unavoidable technical delay. Sometimes, a throwaway song can rise above its humble origins. Jerry Herman wrote the song "Hello, Dolly" to accompany Dolly Levi's triumphal entrance into the Harmonia Gardens. The song was not thrown away. However, when a dramatic situation calls for an establishing number, the composer strives to establish in sound what the lyricist and book writer have already set up in language and dramatic context. For example, Oscar Hammerstein II established in the lyric for "Something Wonderful" *(The King and I)* Lady Thiang's intense love for her husband along with her desperate desire to be to him what she cannot. The opening melodic motif of the song's refrain is a descending sixth interval. In music, the major and minor sixth interval suggests yearning or aspiration. As if to reinforce the point, the composer repeats the interval seven times in the forty-two measures of the refrain. Was it coincidence, skill, luck, forethought, talent, reason, or chance that made the sound of the song the sense of the song? Does it matter? What matters is that it's there, and it works.

Since patter denotes glib, rapid speech, the term *patter song* applies to a song where the composer sets a rapid sequence of compact lyrics to a specific harmonic accompaniment. Patter songs are the recitatives of the popular musical theater but with functions that extend well beyond simple plot exposition. Lyrics dominate the sound of the patter song regardless of function. Their diction, rhythm, and rhyme determine songs of a distinct musical character, one that is more allied to song-speech than song. The recipe for a patter song is this. Set the melodic cadences of accented and richly spoken dialogue to a melodic line of narrow compass; bind all together with a light but driving rhythm. Comedy material fits well into the patter song, particularly when dramatic situation encourages humor generated by incongruity of language.

Where the patter song depends on a rapid delivery of many words made possible in performance by breath support, agility of tongue, and expert diction, the appeal of the *rhythm song* rests on musical values, particularly **212** a dominant musical beat. Rhythm songs induce animated response. Toes tap. Fingers snap. The body moves. Rhythm songs in the early American musical theater were called by the more appropriate name *jump tunes,* and every production featured at least one of these musical whirlwinds that carried away everything on stage in a storm of brisk and lively movement. Time has toned down the "go-for-broke" exuberance of the jump tunes. Still, the tradition lives in the more sophisticated rhythm songs like "Luck Be a Lady Tonight" *(Guys and Dolls)* and the seductive "My Restless Heart" *(Fanny).*

The *chorus number* provides contrast to the solo elements of a musical score. To the lyricist, it offers a framework for the expression of a collective reaction to a dramatic idea or situation. To the composer, it offers the opportunity of use polyphonic vocal harmony with orchestral accompaniment as a forceful aural tool. Invariably, the chorus number projects the population of a show into the spotlight to narrate ("Guinevere" from *Camelot),* bridge a series of dramatic actions ("The Servants' Chorus" from *My Fair Lady),* declaim ("Plain We Live" from *Plain and Fancy),* or celebrate "Oklahoma!" *(Oklahoma!).*

Where the chorus number offers a brief set piece in song, the *musical scene* sets an entire dramatic action to music. Most scores for the serious and ambitious musical play rely on this technique. It is one of the oldest devices peculiar to the musical theater still in active use. Opera and operetta bequeathed it to the popular American musical play where it adapted best to those dramatic situations for which the spoken dialogue alone proved inadequate. Richard Rodgers used the device no less than three times during the score for Act I of *Carousel.* The "If I Loved You" sequence features dialogue that erupts into song on eight separate occasions. Dialogue, singing, and musical interludes cohere into an extended scene where these three forms of musical theater expression flow with no break in the direction of the drama. Although the lyric for the song "If I Loved You" is built along the traditional AABA form, the song itself represents only one unit in the total musical expression of the scene. This musical scene with dialogue transitions develops in the following manner:*

Dialogue
"You're a queer one ...." (Melody 1)
Dialogue transition
"I'm never goin' to marry ...." (Melody 2)
Dialogue transition
"When I worked in the mill ...." (Melody 3)
Dialogue interlude
"If I loved you ...." (Melody 4)
Dialogue transition
"You can't hear a sound ...." (Melody 5)
Monologue over
musical interlude
"There's a helluva lot o' stars ...." (Melody 5)
Dialogue interlude
"Kinda scrawny and pale ...." (Melody 3)
Dialogue interlude
"If I loved you ...." (Melody 4)
Dialogue
Ecstatic musical conclusion ...." (Melody 4)

Integrated into this "scene" are five lyrical patterns, five melodies, monologue, dialogue, and musical interludes. Dramatically, the sequence carries the protagonists from a casual mutual interest to the final kiss that seals their relationship.

Analysis of the design of *Carousel* yields evidence of still another extended sequence of dialogue, lyric, and music integration; the "When the Children Are Asleep" musical scene for Carrie and Mr. Snow. The structure and the motive for this second sequence is the same as the first. The lovers of the subplot are joined, like the lovers of the main plot, through a musical scene that employs adroitly integrated forms of spoken, sung, and sounded expression. Note the structural similarity to its predecessor:**

```
                                    Dialogue
"I own a little house ....................." (Melody 1)
                                    Dialogue
    "If I told you ..........................." (Melody 2)
    "When I make enough money ..........." (Melody 3)
    "All ketchen' herring ..................." (Melody 4)
                                    Dialogue transition
    "When the children are asleep .........." (Melody 5)
    "When children are awake .............." (Melody 1)
    "When the children are asleep .........." (Duet: melody 5)
```

Although structurally related to the first, the second sequence eliminates many of the spoken transitions that link the lyrical-melodic patterns. The effect is operatic. Melodic lines flow into each other without interruption. The musical scene as it evolved in *Carousel* served to move the plot forward, contrast the protagonists with the lovers of the subplot, and point to the dramatic essence of the male comedy character.

Underscoring allows the composer to harness the power of music in an equally soaring but less dramatically specific manner. Unlike incidental music which serves a secondary function by heightening the mood of the drama it accompanies, underscoring represents a highly coordinated effort between composer and librettist to emphasize the dialogue, actions, or scene with which the music coexists. Underscoring is the heightened mood of the theatrical moment, not merely an accompaniment to it. The test? Play a scene without the underscoring. Then play the scene exactly the same way except for the addition of underscoring. The addition doesn't so much accompany what is there as much as it adds something new. In the seconds before the final curtain of *My Fair Lady*, Eliza returns to Henry Higgins, switches off the recording machine, and speaks into the heavily charged silence. At this moment, the orchestra swells into a forceful crescendo from the final measures of "I Could Have Danced All Night." As with this example, appropriate melodic motifs from the score provide the music for the underscoring.

All musicals need to move along at a brisk and rapid pace. Composers of early musical comedy knew this and **215** used the *musical crossover* played in one (a brief song, dance, or comedy excerpt played before the first traveler) to bridge musical scenes. ("First traveler" refers to the transverse curtain closest to the audience, which is opened by being drawn from both sides of the proscenium.) In time, the *segue* replaced the crossover. A segue (pronounced "seg-way") is a brief orchestral passage adapted from music in the preceding scene that pushes the end of a scene into the next. When effective, the segue weaves the distinct parts of a show into a seamless theatrical structure of uninterrupted momentum and accumulating impact.

Have you noticed that composers often bring back a song later in the show to reinforce a point, fill a pause in the action, or add some new dimension to an already-established idea? The device is known as the *reprise,* and its characteristics are these: (1) the reprise should add something and not merely repeat; (2) the reprise should be brief—there is no need to build up material recognized already by the audience; (3) lyrics may or may not change. Commercial motives explain the widespread use of the reprise. Repetition fuels memory. The reprise gives the audience a tune to hum or whistle out of the theater.

Types of Songs

Songs in which the lyric cannot be divorced from the music include ballad, charm song, comedy song, "I am" song, "I want" song, and special material. Most ballads for the musical theater are love songs of simple lyrics and generous melody. As love preoccupies our emotional life, so must a heartfelt tune dominate the lyrics which project that preoccupation. What makes each ballad memorable must be the sound of it, its ability to lift, then transport, through music the most sublime of human feelings. Study a ballad like "We Kiss in a Shadow" *(The King and I)*. Weigh the lyric, then the melody. Doesn't music outweigh lyric?

The charm song stands midway between the ballad and the comedy song. Unlike the ballad where melody 216 predominates, or the comedy song where the lyric rules, the charm song places equal emphasis on music and lyrics. Since the content of a charm song is less determined by precise definition than by a quality conveyed, the charm song category does not exclude other types of song. However, most successful charm songs feature an optimistic content that captivates us, makes us feel good and warm inside. Somewhere between romantic love and outright laughter lives an attitude of deep and secret smiles. The charm song liberates that smile, as did "Happy Talk" *(South Pacific)* and "Do You Love Me?" *(Fiddler on the Roof)*.

Since comedy in the theater grows out of incongruity in life or language, the comedy song makes music subservient to the lyric. A musical joke plays to the orchestra pit; a language joke plays to the audience. Even with this emphasis on lyrics, the music of a comedy song retains a few generally shared characteristics, such as a simple and uncomplicated melodic profile, a complementary rather than dominant quality, and a strong inclination to assume the patter-song personality.

The "eleven o'clock song" originated as special material designed to show off the star minutes before the final curtain. Today, it is the rousing number that stops the show at a point where it no longer needs to get started—that is, near the end. Nothing less than a musical blockbuster will do. Melody, rhythm, and harmony join forces with principals, chorus, and orchestra to end an evening with force and excitement. To create an eleven o'clock song (1) assemble all the combustible materials of music, drama, and theater, and (2) ignite. Sample explosions: "Sit Down, You're Rockin' the Boat" *(Guys and Dolls)* and "Oklahoma!" *(Oklahoma!)*

According to director-choreographer Bob Fosse, songs for the theater fit into additional categories called the "I am" and the "I want" songs. Unlike the types of songs just described, these classifications rest exclusively on the dramatic message of the lyric. The "I am" song establishes something essential to audience understanding of character and situation. The message may be "I feel good about life" ("A Cockeyed Optimist" from *South Pacific*), "I'm in love" ("I Feel Pretty" from *West Side*

Story), or "I am capable of dealing with what appears to be a failed relationship" ("Many a New Day" from *Oklahoma!*). The characters of romantic theater must aspire beyond the position of what they establish in the "I am" song. The "I want" song embodies this aspiration. The "I am" song responds to character and situation; the "I want" song responds to plot. The "I want" song can imply, suggest, or outline a course of action for the character to take. Often, the "I want" song foreshadows the course of action the entire musical show will take. Doesn't the *Camelot* plot respond to Guinevere's wish for the "Simple Joys of Maidenhood"? Doesn't the *Fiddler on the Roof* plot respond to what Tzeitel, Hodel, and Chava want in "Matchmaker"?

Songs classified as *special material* support the special performance talents of the star. These songs can be comic or dramatic, melodic or patter. Sometimes, special material applies to an entire score. Composer Jule Styne designed all the songs for Rose *(Gypsy)* to suit the vocal preferences of Ethel Merman. Special material will be written as long as stars draw audiences into the theater. Unfortunately, special material carries with it a built-in liability. A show whose elements are built to a star's unique gifts may not survive the star's departure.

Elements of a Theater Song

Four elements that figure prominently in an understanding of the theater song are title, function, form, and beat.

The title of a song for the theater should represent something more than a descriptive name of the song's subject. The song *is* the scene in the mature musical theater. Therefore, the song title must address dramatic function, such as the purpose of the scene, the nature of the situation, or the movement in plot, action, or character. To be effective, the title must appear early in the refrain. Such important information must not be buried **218** deep within the text. Oscar Hammerstein II knew this and taught it to Stephen Sondheim. Even in an innovative musical like *Company* where the songs comment on the action rather than further it, the song titles appear early in the refrain. In "The Little Things You Do Together," "Sorry-Grateful," "You Could Drive a Person Crazy," "Have I Got a Girl for You," "Someone Is Waiting," "Another Hundred People," and "The Ladies Who Lunch," the title appears in the first phrase of the lyric. While it is the job of the lyricist to determine a title appropriate to dramatic purpose, the composer must respond by setting title to an appropriate musical motif. The short-note percussive quality of the musical setting of the word *company* reflects the rhythm of the setting and the tone of the entire show. Similarly, Sondheim set the twin phrases "You're always sorry, you're always grateful" to musical phrases similar enough to establish the near-agreement and balance between those two extremes yet varied enough in melody and harmony to make the tune aurally attractive.

If there really is a difference between a popular song and a theater song, what is it? While both can be appreciated for their own sake, the theater song exists to fulfill a dramatic or theatrical function. The composer draws from some of the following alternatives. First, the music of a theater song can project character. Nellie Forbush *(South Pacific)* is a roller coaster of a personality who rides many emotional highs and lows in her love affair with Emile de Becque. Richard Rodgers built into the melodic profile of "A Wonderful Guy" the musical equivalent of Nellie's personality. The notes of the refrain jump up and down the melodic scale just as if a flowchart of the character's fluctuating inner movements somehow found its way onto the musical scale. Second, the music of a theater song can intensify emotion. While lyrics provide a precise indication of what a character is feeling or thinking, music can transport that content beyond the capability of spoken sound. Often, theater songs have a melodic profile characterized by a broad rising melodic curve that carries with it an emotional intensity whose heightened climax generates emotional release. All great

musical theater composers from Kern to Sondheim build

Richard Rodgers wrote his most dramatic melodies with a broad and rising melodic profile. The finale—"You'll Never Walk Alone," *Carousel,* 1945. (Photo: The Lynn Farnol Group, Inc.)

songs on this phenomenon. The rising melodic line of "Ol' Man River" or "You'll Never Walk Alone" conceals a built-in bomb that explodes in a theatrical climax far more exciting than what even the most skilled performer could achieve speaking the lines. Third, theater song music can create dramatic images. The concept of program music rests on an acceptance of the assumption that music can summon up a mental picture. The image of the surrey with the fringe on top hovers over the opening dramatic situation of *Oklahoma!* While the surrey itself doesn't appear during the scene, its image must appear in Laurey's imagination. Richard Rodgers responded to the task by joining a regular rhythm to repeated staccato notes for the "clippety-cloppety, clippety-cloppety" quality of a moving surrey. Fourth, theater song music can be created to embody theme. *Fiddler on the Roof* is about tradition. Tevye's dialogue tells us so, but so does the com-

220

poser, especially in the consistent use of half-tone intervals in melody and harmony. It may be that a half-tone ascending melodic interval that returns to the tonic suggests a musical peculiarity of Eastern European song. Whatever the origin, or interpretation, the device, once established, returns again and again to remind the audience what the musical is about. The half-tone appears first as a descending melodic interval in the "Dai, dai, dai, dai" musical figure of "Tradition." In the religious expression of that tradition embodied in the "Sabbath Prayer," the half-tone interval ascends and descends on the words ". . . God bless you" and "And grant you. . . ." Here the composer also adds a harmonic variation achieved by diminishing the third tone by one half-step on the harmony for the word *grant*. During the scene of Tzeitel's marriage to Motel, a dramatic manifestation of the social aspects of the tradition, all who are embraced by the tradition sing "Sunrise, Sunset," where the half-tone descending melodic interval again figures prominently in the opening measures of the refrain. Fifth, the music of a theater song can suggest time and place. When the allusive power of rhythm, harmony, and melody combines with the descriptive power of language and the visual stimuli of design, the musical theater generates a unique dramatic moment unlikely to occur in any other form of theater, and from whose assault on the emotions there is no defense.

Song Forms

The evolution of song forms into variations of the AABA pattern within the verse-and-refrain framework accounts for much of what the mature theater song has been able to accomplish. Minstrelsy and vaudeville were vigorous and popular forms of musical entertainment that dominated American show business in their time. Songs were used rarely for anything more ambitious than vocal display or dance accompaniment because the typical song structure of the period proved too weak to support more ambitious objectives. "Polly Wolly Doodle" (1855), one of the most performed songs of the minstrel troupes, offers no more than a verse, melodic motif A, and a refrain, melodic motif B. For "Buffalo Gals" (1850), the composer employs verse A with repetition, and chorus B with repetition. Even the best examples of what were then called "Ethiopian" songs, like "My Old Kentucky Home" (1854), relied on the brief verse A, A and refrain B, A. Structurally, vaudeville songs fare better, but not by much. Although longer in verse and melody, the structural stereotypes persisted, as in "Sidewalks of New York" (1894) with verse A, A and refrain B, A, and "In the Good Old Summertime," verse A, A and refrain B, B. Today the most traditional and persistent song form for the theater employs this pattern:

> VERSE (Secondary Importance)
> **A** Statement of initial melody of the verse
> **B** Statement of a complementary melody of the verse
>
> REFRAIN (Primary Importance)
> **A** Statement of initial melody of the refrain
> **A** Repetition of the initial melody of the refrain
> **B** Entirely new and contrasting melody (Not the same as the B in the verse.)
> **A** Final repetition of initial melody of the refrain

This framework and its refrain variations AABB, ABAB, and ABAC allow the songwriter to attach patterns of dramatic development to repeated patterns of sound and so bring dramatic meaning to songs that might otherwise have aspired to nothing beyond pure entertainment.

Theater songs rely on the song beats indicated by the time signature to reveal the song's function within the structural framework. All time signatures derive from two major song beats, the duple or 2/4 and the triple or 3/4. All others are multiples of the basic two. To execute duple time, allow two beats to the measure and accent every other beat. Duple time is up-tempo and, in theater songs, suggestive of all that is light, lively, exciting, and just plain show-biz. To execute triple time, allow three beats to the measure and accent every third beat. Triple time is waltz time. Common time or 4/4 lengthens the rhythm of 2/4 to include four beats to the measure **222** with the primary accent on the downbeat and a secondary accent on the third beat. Romantic ballads find the slow and expansive quality so generated most suitable for lush and generous melody. To execute a 6/8 rhythm, allow six beats to the measure with a primary accent on the first beat and a secondary accent on the fourth beat. While rock scores use traditional beats, the rock drive comes not from the use of common time rhythm but from the stylistic disposition to accent every beat.

Although the American popular song emerged long before the mature musical theater book, the mature concept of a musical theater score developed simultaneously with the latter. Many composers write songs for the musical theater, but few of them write musical theater songs. As long as the American musical theater honors the Kern-Rodgers-Sondheim accomplishment and instructs from the principles they demonstrated, the tradition of the mature American musical score will be preserved.

13

DANCE

The images of dance surround us in life and art. Bodies in rhythmic movement burst out at us at parties, nightclubs, discos, television entertainments, magazines, newspaper advertisements, and movies. Museums offer no refuge. Botticelli painted dance. So did Breughel, Rubens, Degas, Monet, Goya, and Picasso. French peasants wheel about a fifteenth-century manuscript, satyrs and maenads leap around an Attic vase, men dance on the walls of Etruscan tombs, women dance on the walls of Egyptian tombs—our past is recorded in images of dance as old even as the androgynous figures who float through the neolithic drawings from the Hoggar Mountains of the Sahara. Man's fascination with dance stems from the preoccupation of the living with the signals and symbols of life. If movement separates the living from the dead, then controlled rhythmic movement celebrates that separation. I move, therefore I am. Where there is life, there is dance. Where there is joy, there is dance. Where there is hope, religion, society, art, and drama, there is dance. Dora Stratou, the foremost authority on the restoration of ancient Greek dances, assigns no mystery to the phenomenon. After all, isn't dance "the most direct expression of human feelings and sentiment . . . ?" On the validity of that observation rests the philosophy, functions, and importance of dance in the musical theater.

All the artistic principles of thought and conduct that regulate the musical theater issue from the conviction that musicals typify romantic theater in content and

225 form. Since the romantic theater tradition spends arrows

aimed directly at the heart, most popular musicals in the American theater celebrate dramatic moments of intense feeling with song. Until recently, dance was locked into a position of decorous and entertaining adjunct. Today, dance assumes a more prominent place in the creative and interpretative process, often bearing dramatic and theatrical responsibilities equal to book, lyrics, and music. And why not? Dance symbols can be as effective as language or music symbols for dramatic communication. What sets dance apart is the universality in movement and gesture which is not bound like language to nationality or culture. Dance transcends geography in a way that language cannot. Dance humanizes expression in a way that music cannot. Harold Prince chose Jerome Robbins to direct *Fiddler on the Roof* because he sensed the need for a director-choreographer who could tell a story of Russian Jews in the universal language of dance.

Elements

Dance cannot define, explain, determine, or prescribe, but like music, dance can suggest. It directs appeals to the imagination with conscious symbolic statements made through the extraordinary communicative power of dance forms, patterns, dynamics, styles, and virtuosity.

Form in dance represents the shape of the whole, that is, the structure of the dance in time. Like the lyric which exists in time, dance form submits to organizational principles like beginning, middle, and end, or theme, variation, and restatement. For instance, a dance in the service of *West Side Story* might begin with a meeting: Tony and Maria enter from opposite sides of the stage and meet during the dance at the gym. Their attraction may develop during a middle section where they dance together, and end when dramatic situation forces them to retreat to opposite sides of the stage.

Within form, dance communicates through a systematic arrangement of position and step elements known as *pattern.* Lyrics reflect pattern in rhythm and rhyme. **226**

Music reflects pattern in the rhythm of song beats. Dance reflects pattern in planned combinations of flowing or accented steps in symmetry or asymmetry. Three ingredients constitute pattern: the step, the combination, the arrangement. A step involves the action of body movement that is brought to rest again. A combination involves joining together a series of steps. Arrangement involves an organization of dancers performing the combinations. A symmetrical arrangement creates a restful and aesthetically pleasing image through the similar arrangement of dancers on both sides of a real or imaginary line. To make Maria and Tony enter from opposite sides of the stage and meet facing each other on both sides of the imaginary line that divides the stage in half is to suggest a pleasing and peaceful moment during what will soon become an arena of explosive conflict. Asymmetrical patterns stimulate restless, exciting images through an unbalanced arrangement of dancers. Generally, formal and decorous dances favor symmetry; spontaneous and violent dances favor asymmetry.

Those who dance the patterns within the form submit to principles of *dynamics* that control the relative force exerted by bodies in motion. The dynamics of music regulate the degrees of volume in performance; the dynamics of dance regulate the degrees of kinesthetic strength and weakness regulated by the choreography. Dynamic variations bring to dance the contrasts most apparent to an audience: moments of energy, vigor, and power contrasted to moments of weakness, frailty, and calm.

Style makes a statement independent of dynamics. Style is the specific manner of expression peculiar to a work, a period, or a personality. It implies the purposeful and consistent choice of expressive ingredients to achieve a characteristic manner. In the musical theater, dance styles speak most often to the period of the show, the talent of the choreographer, or the tone of the material, whichever value rises most in the pecking order of collaborative priorities. Some choreographers adapt their talent to the material; others adapt the material to the talent. Jerome Robbins took the former course in *Fiddler on the Roof*; Bob Fosse took the latter in *Pippin* and *Chicago*.

A dance style is the specific manner of expression peculiar to a work achieved by the purposeful and consistent choice of expressive ingredients. *The Hot Mikado,* 1939. (Photo: Theatre and Music Collection, Museum of the City of New York)

Only after settling on form, pattern, dynamics, and style do serious choreographers turn to performance *virtuosity* to generate audience excitement. While dance in the mature musical theater exists to serve the book, dance steps and combinations can and do draw attention to themselves, particularly when an exceptionally talented dancer defies the laws of balance and gravity to meet the demands of the choreography. In the presentational world of the American musical, controlled virtuosity works like an effective song: both stimulate applause.

Language

From the general foundation provided by the elements of dance, theater choreography services the book through a vocabulary and grammar that embrace body positions, simple movements, turns, jumps, and gestures. By devising a dramatically purposeful statement in images drawn **228** from this dance alphabet, the theater choreographer can fashion a unit of communication as effective in the theater as a scene, a lyric, or a song. In this sense, the mechanics of the choreographer resemble the mechanics of the writer. Each builds words, notes, or *steps* into sentences, melodic motifs, or *combinations* that coalesce into a scene, a song, or a *dance*. The range of expression in dance images corresponds to the range of expression in music and literature; only the symbols are different.

The variety of dance images grow from the number and sequence of steps a choreographer chooses from the many available symbols in the language of dance. Consider the steps and combinations that flow from the five principal positions of the leg: sole, ball, point, heel, and flowing position (one foot lifted off the floor). In each, the positions can be open or closed, inward-turned or in air, bended or stretched. Simple movements accomplish the transitions from one position to another. These involve the motions of bending, stretching, raising, lowering, lifting, turning, or transferring. Accompanying arm positions can be horizontal at the sides, vertical or perpendicular, stretched or bent in any of the five degrees of bending, open or closed. Hands can be presented palm upward or downward, inward toward the body or outward. Jumping or movement through the air can take the character of hopping, springing, raising, or throwing. From the endless combinations of units from this vocabulary do choreographers form the dances that serve the special demands of each mature Broadway musical.

Origins

The dance of primitive self-expression and religious ritual adapted early and well to service in the civilized theater. Modern students of Cretan culture assure us that one thousand years before the Dionysian festivals, music and dance entertainments pleasured audiences in the court theaters of Phaestus and Knossus. In ancient Greece, dance accompanied tragedy, comedy, and the satyr plays. Rome favored a dance-drama known as pantomime. Although the Church labored vigorously for over one thousand years to suppress "this evil, this lascivious madness in man called dance," the Middle Ages proved to be alive with dances like the macabre and communal "dance of death" that swept Europe during the years of the bubonic plague. Important distinctions emerge in the late Middle Ages between the earthy, spontaneous dances of the people and the regulated and refined dances of the nobility. From the former developed the traditions and materials of folk dance; from the latter grew the forms and character of theater dance. Generally, folk dance forms embody the spontaneous expression of joyous emotion performed by *all* to the vocal accompaniment of the participants. Theater dance represents a controlled expression of refined ideas performed by designated individuals in predetermined patterns to instrumental accompaniment. As the masquerades, madrigals, and pageants of the Middle Ages grew into the extravagant and spectacular entertainments of the Renaissance nobility, dance assumed a more important place in the theatrical event. When Catherine de Medici settled in France as wife to King Henry II, she brought with her the concept of the *ballet* as a refined and involved art of figured movement. Although it originated in northern Italy, the form developed in France into a theatrical entertainment of the court known as the "ballet de cour." None was more famous or important to the history of theater dance than the *Ballet Comique de la Reine* (1581), the earliest recorded incidence of acting, music, and dance in the service of a dramatic idea. Staged for a ceremonious occasion, the ballet told the story of Circe to ten thousand guests of the royal court in a spectacle that lasted five-and-one-half hours. Since the ballet was an integrated musical entertainment that employed dance as a vital instrument in the total expression of the theatrical idea, it represents to theater dance what opera represents to musical theater: the archetype from which all subsequent forms would issue.   **230**

Dramatic Functions

Once a creative collaboration determines the amount and place of dance in the concept of a show, the choreographer in the service of the book is free to investigate its use in the following ways.

TO CARRY PLOT

Where the nonlyric theater employs dialogue and action to carry the plot to another logical stage of development, the musical theater relies on song or movement. The "Dream Ballet" that concludes Act I of *Oklahoma!* takes the plot from Laurey's indecision to an action whose motive the ballet reveals only to the audience. When a show needs a rapid forward movement of the plot, dance can initiate, advance, or complete the desired dramatic action. In *West Side Story,* Jerome Robbins used dance to initiate conflict between the Jets and the Sharks in the "Prologue," advance the conflict during "The Dance at the Gym," and complete the action during "The Rumble." If needed, dance can telescope the action of the plot, that is, carry it some distance in a disproportionate amount of time. Through a dance sequence of only forty measures of music, Tony and Maria see each other during "The Dance at the Gym," approach, and fall in love, an action that could have taken pages of dialogue to develop.

TO ESTABLISH
MOOD OR ATMOSPHERE

Mood submits readily to dance expression because the human body registers in muscular tension and movement the visible impact of thought and emotion on a character. Since strong emotions like joy or sadness register quickly in facial expression, posture, or gesture, their re-creation in dance art is likely to transmit clear signals to an audi-

231

ence eager to participate in the theatrical event. Although music reinforces the atmosphere, it is the dancer's body, alone or in combination with others', that gives visual expression to the impact of the surrounding environment on the character. Dance expression can provoke violent shifts of mood, too. In *Brigadoon*, dance carries the show from the lively and joyful country dance directly into the ritual mourning of the "Funeral Dance."

TO EMBODY
THEME OR IDEA

Among the revolutionary accomplishments of *Oklahoma!* was the discovery that the techniques of dance could be used to project the ideas of the book with no loss in dramatic credibility or suspension of audience disbelief. If a song can be a scene, why can't a dance be a scene? Rodgers and Hammerstein assigned Act II, Scene 3 of *The King and I* to the ballet sequence "The Small House of Uncle Thomas," where a stylized dance-narration of *Uncle Tom's Cabin* exhibits in microcosm the musical play's twin themes of slavery and oppression.

TO REPLACE DIALOGUE

When musical theater collaborators explore the alternatives to dialogue for projecting the elements of the book, two possibilities occur: song and dance. Songs replace dialogue with compact language set to music; dance replaces dialogue with images of movement set to music. The advantage of dance? Movement forwards *action* more naturally than language. Multisecond dance sequences can equal multiminute book scenes in weight or scope of dramatic action. Consequently, dance accounts for the brevity of the action-packed *West Side Story* book, the most concise text in the repertory of great musicals.

TO GENERATE COMEDY

Although both issue best from incongruity in dramatic situation, the true comedy of movement is more difficult 232 to sustain on the stage than the conventional comedy of language. The reason: it is more in the nature of language to register the clash between the setup (expectation) and the punch (unsuspected fulfillment) that provokes the laughter response. To generate laughter, the choreographer must set up a visual situation and build into it an unsuspected visual response to elicit audience laughter. Visual images are more difficult to achieve in surprise situations than language. A word can pop out anytime; not so a body or prop. No maker of dances has been more successful at comedy choreography than Jerome Robbins. You can study the phenomenon of dance comedy in his ballet *The Concert,* the "Keystone Cops Ballet" *(High Button Shoes),* and "Tevye's Dream" *(Fiddler on the Roof).*

TO EXTEND
A DRAMATIC MOMENT

When the cumulative development of a well-constructed book arrives at a moment of critical importance to the life of a musical show, the need usually arises to keep the audience there. Dance can extend that moment. It transports even the simplest point of development up and out, only to return it to the same place without recourse to repetition or reprise. Tony and Maria meet, dance, fall in love, set the plot on its inevitable course. When the dance ends, Tony and Maria return to the initial situation of having just met. Much has happened in that extended theatrical moment; yet nothing has happened in the plot beyond the fact that they've met. Used in this way, dance adds an emotional dimension without diverting the flow of the drama.

TO OVERWHELM
IN SPECTACLE

No device in the musical theater is more apt to generate the kinesthetic excitement that constitutes true spectacle than dance reinforced by sets, costumes, and lighting. Today, the American public is spectator to a variety of

physical wonders in televised sports where the marvel

of technology allows all to languish over the virtuosity of athletes frozen in flight by instant replay. A nation of kinesthetic voyeurs accustomed to the increasing show-biz spectacle of sports merchandising demands no less from the popular arts than it expects from the popular pastimes. The American musical theater has grown with its public. The dance spectacle that was once an attractive garnish now constitutes an essential ingredient in the preparation of the dish. In the most recent work of direc-tor-choreographers like Jerome Robbins, Bob Fosse, and Michael Bennett, spectacular theater dance makes a par-allel, not a supplementary, contribution to the modern musical show.

Types

Choreography in the service of a musical book relies on dances whose character, plan, structure, and develop-ment identify them as opening number, solo, duet, male or female ensemble, production number, ballet sequence, and crossover.

Although the opening number evolved from the "bring on the girls in a lively routine" formula of early musical comedy, its place and function in the serious mod-ern musical theater eschews cheap entertainment for the opportunity to demonstrate to the audience in physical terms the who, what, when, where, and how of the show to follow. The Jerome Robbins choreography for "Tradi-tion" *(Fiddler on the Roof)* gives physical form to the show's immediate answer to each question.

Performed by one person alone, the solo dance ad-vances a single idea or character. When the soloist repre-sents the community, the *solo* dance speaks symbolically for all who matter in the world on the stage. The solo dance offers an additional advantage to the choreogra-pher: The special gifts of the best dancer can be used in patterns and combinations too difficult or ambitious for the ensemble.

With romantic love a staple in the musical theater, **234**

choreographers cannot afford to ignore the possibilities of the *duet*, a dance composition for two performers. What language can only signify of the physical character of a relationship, dance can establish through concrete images recognizable to the senses. Complementary body positions, harmonious movement, and affectionate gesture are themselves the expressions of romantic love, not merely symbols, like language, once removed from the fact. However, not all duets are amorous. Any relationship that permits physical expression invites choreographic treatment.

Audiences accept *male* or *female ensemble* dances as an inevitable dance category because human beings tend to congregate in sexually exclusive groups for special activities, social functions, and entertainment. Since conflict must delay the inevitable romantic resolution for nearly the entire length of most musical shows, male and female group dances offer opportunities for support, comment, or contrast to both sides of the battle between the sexes.

In the *production number,* the entire dance ensemble contributes to purposeful spectacle. The production number represents the choreographer's most collabora-

Dances for the female ensemble have always been a hallmark of the musical stage. *Fiddle-Dee-Dee,* 1900. (Photo: Byron, The Byron Collection, Museum of the City of New York)

In the production number, the entire dance ensemble contributes to purposeful spectacle. "The Farmer and the Cowman," *Oklahoma!* 1943. (Photo: The Lynn Farnol Group, Inc.)

tive effort as dance joins music, lyrics, performers, set, costumes, and orchestration in a joyous and full musical theater moment.

Dance becomes the ally of plot in the *ballet sequence*. This type of dance can precipitate action ("The Dream Ballet" in *Oklahoma!*), comment on situation ("Ballet Sequence" in *West Side Story*), or advance an argument ("Small House of Uncle Thomas" in *The King and I*). When the choreographer must devise dances that divert the audience from unavoidable technical problems, these brief dances performed before a downstage drop curtain are called *crossovers*.

Dance has become as vital as song to the makeup of the mature American musical. While styles of dance may change—from tap to modified ballet to jazz/show dance—dance itself has never been out of fashion. Consider this selective roster of choreographers who have shaped dance images for the Broadway musical since the **236**

1930s: George Balanchine, Agnes de Mille, Jerome Robbins, Michael Kidd, Bob Fosse, and Michael Bennett. Their legacy is considerable both as entertainment and as art. It deserves to be studied by all who participate in the American musical theater just as it must command the attention of anyone interested in the American scene. "Theater dance," said the late dancer-choreographer Jack Cole, "is the way the American dancer expresses his culture, his understanding of his time."

14

DESIGN

While all design artists draw from the same well of principles, materials, and techniques, two ideals so stand out in design for the musical theater that they constitute the basis for its unique design philosophy. First, musical theater aspires to the total theater objective of the "concentrated activation" of sound, color, space, form, and movement. The ultimate duty of design for the musical theater is to serve that idea. Second, the nature of the evolution of a musical show allows the designer to be included in the process of creative collaboration. Unlike his counterpart in the nonlyric theater who *interprets* the finished play, the design artist for the musical theater can help *create* the emerging musical. Let's examine these ideals before we explore that well of basic design principles, materials, and techniques.

A Philosophy

If scenery is environment in the modern theater, then the ultimate objective of the designer of musicals must be to service the moving forms that characterize the musical theater. Everything moves in an effective musical: musical notes, lyrics, actors, dancers, scenes, scenery. Consider the movement of the book to which the designer must respond. The majority of modern musicals 239 develop according to a multiscene structural format.

Company takes eleven scenes in two acts, *West Side Story* fifteen scenes in two acts, *Fiddler on the Roof* eighteen scenes in two acts, and *South Pacific* twenty-four scenes in two acts. An effective design must not only accommodate numerous changes of locale but account for fluid transitions as well. In addition, the design concept must take into account unrelenting movement within this moving structure—the movement precipitated by an obvious ingredient: music. The rhythm indicated by the time signature regulates the music, specifically, the patterns of strong and weak beats that carry the music along in time. In the nonlyric theater, director and performer regulate pace. In the musical theater, the rhythm of the music determines the pace. The movement in music generates other movement which characterizes what the audience in musical theater hears and sees. It regulates the flow of the lyric, the movement of the performer, the blocking of the director, and the choreography for the dancers. These features must concern the designer in that the music of musical theater parcels the time of a show into units (songs) that regulate their performers in space. As the composer regulates what the audience hears, so does the designer regulate what the audience sees as it hears.

Unlike representational design for the theater of realism where appropriate environments mean credible visual backgrounds that condition character and situation, presentational designs for the musical theater celebrate the theatrical artifice of the event and strive for an aesthetic unity through the harmony of all the creative aspects of the production. Where the former concentrates on the "significant trifle," that is, the imitation of the specific, particularized surface aspects of the play's experience, the latter eschews detailed appearances for a broader artistic purpose that would account for the performer. Effective musical theater design bypasses reality in order to set in relief the ultimate reality of the musical stage: the singing, moving, dancing actor. Adolphe Appia originated this design philosophy. His convictions led him to dismiss painted stage setting as incompatible with true theatrical art because of the lack of aesthetic harmony between a moving, three-dimensional actor and the painted, two-dimensional surroundings. Modern design- **240**

Design for the musical theater bypasses reality in order to set in relief the ultimate reality of the musical stage—the singing, moving, dancing actor. Model of production designed by Donald Oenslager for *I'd Rather Be Right*, 1937. (Photo: Theatre and Music Collection, Museum of the City of New York)

ers for the musical theater reflect Appia's principles in the pictorial manner of their work, avoiding the too rigid and precise compositional techniques of the easel painters which would war inevitably with the moving performers. If effective musical theater design acts as a relief to the reality instead of being the reality itself, then the suggestive, fuzzy, colorful, and decorative artists serve as the best models for musical theater pictorial design. We see the lesson learned by Boris Aronson, whose designs in the style of Marc Chagall frame the considerable movement in *Fiddler on the Roof*. As a form of romantic theater, musical theater tends to value emotion over intellect, passion over decorum, and illusion over reality. Only when the designer abandons accurate visual symbolizing for a free imagination dedicated to the expressive function of his art will his product serve the best interests of the musical theater form.

While the steps for formulating and drafting a design remain the same in the lyric and nonlyric theater, the process of *creative collaboration* for the designer of the Broadway musical extends throughout the rehearsal and out-of-town tryout period, during which the design artist

241

functions as creative coequal to the writer, composer, lyricist, director, and choreographer. Whereas most successful plays are complete going into rehearsal, most musicals undergo radical change during the evolutionary period known as "out of town." Although plays undergo rewrites on the road, the changes are usually cosmetic and rarely affect the design component. Not so in the American musical theater. Even the most foresighted musical theater creative collaboration cannot avoid radical changes out-of-town. Ask Stephen Sondheim about the creative evolution of the opening for *A Funny Thing Happened on the Way to the Forum* that cost the producer $50,000.

Procedures

The unique contribution a designer makes to the musical theater evolves through a design procedure described in the nine consecutive phases which follow. The first five steps cover the period of creative collaboration where design enters actively into the making of a musical show. The final four steps cover the period where design assumes a more interpretative function. It is to be understood that this procedure is subject to the individual variations that come along with the personalities, working methods, concept, materials, time, and budget of each show.

STEP 1:
STAFF HIRED ON ROUGH SCRIPT

Usually, the designer contracts his services in the nonlyric theater after reading a completed manuscript. His services are more likely to be secured for a musical theater project on the basis of an author's outline, a few scenes, and a couple of songs. Although the entire procedure begins with an air of indefiniteness, a stimulating prospect looms ahead: active participation in the creative evolution of a show. An experienced and imaginative designer 242 can meter a surprising number of creative vibrations from fragments and crumbs offered by his collaborators. An outline can convey what William and Jean Eckert call the "essence" of the material. A scene or two can convey the "flavor" of the material. A song can convey the "feel" of the show. From this initial contact with the material, the designer should be able to sense a preliminary design idea, one that sees the basics of the show from a visual standpoint. Here each designer operates according to personal convictions. A designer might try to visualize the most dramatic and intense scenes and extract a central scenic motif from each. Another might try to discover the essence of the material, then support and extend it from a visual standpoint. Another might try to visualize the performers in important situations that yield clues to the cornerstone for the entire setting. However vague such activity appears to the laymen, this process of rough reflection is a prerequisite to the next step.

STEP 2:
THE INITIAL PRODUCTION MEETING

After confronting the rough script, writer, lyricist, composer, director, choreographer, designer, and producer gather for mutual responses to ideas and problems. Active participation in the discussions at this phase of planning and development allows the designer to exercise creative muscle in decisions that will determine what the audience must see and how they must see it. Initial differences of philosophy and interpretation must be resolved before concerted work on specific problems can continue. Only then does the collaborative team address its energies to structural problems like breaking the musical down into types of scenes (intimate scenes, action scenes, solo songs, production numbers, crossovers). At this stage, the designer should be able to determine the number and kinds of settings his design concept must accommodate. Here, additional information may be made available to him, like the space requirements of the director or choreographer, the number and pattern of interior and exterior scenes, and the amount and specific placement of songs

243

and dances. Only then does the designer abandon collaborative interaction for the relative seclusion of research.

STEP 3:
RESEARCH

Professional designers engage in exhaustive research to help extend their visual images of the essence, feel, or quality inherent in the evolving show. Talent alone does not sustain a serious career in theater design. The craft is served best by knowledge reinforced with an experience of the material. Research libraries stocked with vast files of photographs, graphics, memorabilia, clippings, and general literature assist the purposeful researcher acquire a sense of period, locale, and style. Personal files can direct the artist to earlier efforts, problems, and solutions. Specific and unfocused interviews provide an added source of the facts and opinions that broaden outlook and suggest new avenues of information. Since most librettists adapt musical shows from previously successful plays, the researcher should not neglect the original author, director, or cast members as potential sources of factual or interpretative data. If the designer is a sensitive and sensible creative artist, he will take ideas wherever he finds them. After all, creative interaction that leads to mutual influence distinguishes the collaborative process. Nor must travel be discounted as a source of artistic stimulation. The most honest and convincing art emerges from what the artist knows best—the sensations of what has been actually seen, heard, smelled, tasted, done, and believed. While no attempt will be made in the musical theater to reproduce the images of direct experience, the absorbed sensations may fuel the insight and perspective needed to ignite the fires of a vivid imagination. Unfortunately, the research period can be a time-consuming and artistically frustrating period, one that is lonely and full of hard work without the satisfaction of a concrete product to justify time and effort.

STEP 4:
STAFF CONFERENCES

Homework completed, the designer confronts his collaborators in work sessions designed to weigh the preliminary **244** design concept against the show's specific production requirements. Here the director should present demands as to the nature and amount of stage space required for each scene, a suggested floor plan of entrances, exits, and levels, a tentative arrangement of furniture or props, and an opinion on production values to be emphasized. The producer should submit a budget, the assets and liabilities of the theater to be used, and an inventory of the available equipment. These work sessions must produce concrete results, that is, planned patterns of movement and dance, specific dimensions, suggested colors, and mutual agreement on style—data that frames the interpretative, physical, and financial world of the designer until the show is frozen prior to opening.

STEP 5:
"SEESAW"

Gradually, the staff-conferences period blends into what Howard Bay calls "seesaw," the period of compromise and adjustment. Here, writers, composer, lyricist, director, choreographer, designer, and producer face the ultimate challenge of collaboration: how to achieve that delicate balance between enlightened self-interest and the good of the whole. The infamous arguments, hysteria, bitterness, and squabbling that threaten even the best-intentioned collaboration surface at this stage. To survive, the designer must rely on an open mind, a strong heart, an even disposition, and a willingness to compromise. There can be no place in seesaw for excessive self-indulgence, exhibitional digressions, inflexible attitudes, and the cult of personality. Everyone must concentrate on one primary objective: the total concept of the show pushing forward to a unique destination. Usually, seesaw proves a mixed blessing, a period of personal trauma mixed with creative accomplishment. Barriers between disciplines fall. Artists share once-exclusive interests and responsibilities. A choreographer may take a book scene and replace it with a telescopic ballet. The director may stumble on an appropriate scenic motif. The designer may see a vital dramatic moment in such overwhelming visual terms as to inspire the composer and lyricist to write a new and better song. Seesaw ends the period of intensive creative collaboration for the designer. The next step? The drawing board.

STEP 6:
THE DRAWING BOARD

After the intense collaborative interaction of the seesaw period, the designer retreats to the seclusion of the drawing board to execute the hanging plot, rough sketches, floor plans, and three-dimensional model specified in his contract. The preliminary hanging plot deserves top priority. It diagrams the positions of all the hanging and standing units, charts the operation of the design, and determines the light plot. To show how the settings will look on stage, the designer must sketch color renderings in perspective. Ground plans in $\frac{1}{4}$-inch- or $\frac{1}{2}$-inch-per-foot scale accompany the renderings. Their purpose? To give the director the specific physical dimensions only implied in the color sketch. Since stage art happens in a three-dimensional medium, the scale model represents the truest indication of how the design idea will appear on stage. What can the director determine from a miniaturized model? Spacial composition, relationships between performers and scenery, angles of sight lines, form, mass,

Since stage art happens in a three-dimensional medium, the scale model represents the truest indication of how the design will appear on stage. Oliver Smith's model for the Great Hall, finale of Act I, *Camelot*. (Photo: Theatre and Music Collection, Museum of the City of New York)

and depth. The drawing board yields specific designs. Some will be accepted; others will be rejected. Only after final approval of all materials does the designer address the final task of preparing working drawings for shop construction.

STEP 7:
WORKING DRAWINGS

After the director's final approval, the designer initiates the building phase with working drawings that guide scenery construction. While scale of $\frac{1}{2}$-inch per foot is standard in the nonlyric theater, the sheer size of musical theater designs encourages drawings to the scale of $\frac{1}{4}$-inch per foot. Depending on director preference or contractual agreement, the designer may be required to submit the following:

1. *Color sketches of each setting as it appears to the audience.* Drawn in perspective, the sketch should indicate how the setting will look in stage lighting. The sketches can be rendered in pastels, colored pencils, chalk, oil paints, water colors, acrylics, tempera, or gouache. William and Jean Eckart used children's crayons for the sketches for *Fiorello* because crayons helped express the crude, forceful, childlike quality of the main character.

2. *Color elevations that indicate to the builder what each piece of scenery should look like.* In a musical, color elevations should accompany the wings, drops, groundcloths, units, major props, and important set dressing. Should the designer create a color model with removable scenery, sections of the model can be used as paint elevations. In any case, the painter's elevations must be drawn to scale, indicate actual color, and signal a specific painting technique.

3. *A model in scale that shows in three dimensions each piece of scenery and how all units relate to each other and the total stage space.* While models can be built to scales $\frac{1}{4}$-inch per foot, $\frac{3}{8}$-inch per foot, or 1 inch per foot, most professional designers for the musical theater prefer the scale of $\frac{1}{2}$-inch per foot.

4. *A ground plan for each setting that shows from above the scenery as it appears on the stage floor.* Drafting ground plans is an essential responsibility of the professional designer and his assistants, as it provides the most accurate measure of the technical aspects of the scenery, information that is vital to the director, the lighting designer, the technical director, the carpenters, the scenic artists, the stage manager, and property men. Most drafting for the Broadway musical is done in $\frac{1}{2}$-inch-per-foot scale.

247

5. *Front and/or side and/or rear elevations.* These elevations show each unit in two dimensions as it appears from the front, side, and rear, respectively. In the front elevation, each piece of scenery appears in a flat, elongated view so dimensioned as to aid the carpenter in building. The rear-view working drawings show the carpenter how to build the scenery from behind. These drawings direct the shop in scenery construction without the physical presence of the designer.

STEP 8:
DESIGNER APPROVAL

While the designer need not be present during the period of shop construction, it is his responsibility to be sure that the finished product conforms to the style and specifications of his drawings. The designer may make visits to the scene shop when time allows and may actually be present to add the finishing touches. It is expected that the designer will be available to answer any questions about interpretation and construction, make appropriate adjustment, and offer final approval. When approval is granted, the scenery can be taken from the shop, stored, or loaded for travel to the preview or out-of-town destination.

STEP 9:
PREVIEWS OR OUT OF TOWN

The designer of a musical reenters the collaborative process during the farrago of previews or out-of-town opening. Rewriting and rearranging can force substantial design revisions. Often, the drama-surgery demands nothing more than scenery substitution. Where weaknesses cannot be so corrected, the collaboration must initiate new materials from new ideas. It can be hectic—chaotic even. When the musical succeeds, the designer can take credit for having had a hand in shaping the product. When it fails, he must share the blame.

Elements

All design for the theater makes use of basic materials, principles, and techniques. Let's consider these elements **248** prior to our survey of the design formats most suitable to the musical stage.

The designers of the modern theater pursue a common objective: to create a performance environment that reflects the production concept of the director. That environment can make a visual statement about theme, character, mood, tone, language, structure, or style. To be effective, the settings must go beyond the mere account of time and place. Scenery creates the visual world of the play, not just the background for it.

THE MATERIALS OF DESIGN

All art relies on materials which the artist's craft molds into the statement embodied in the painting, the sonata, the sculpture, or the dramatic characterization. The materials of the composer? Melody, harmony, rhythm. The materials of the actor? Voice, body, mind, emotion. The materials of the designer? Space, line, form, color, texture.

Space. The theater is a place as well as an idea, a place of three-dimensional distances subject to the occupation of mass and the movement of actors. How the designer chooses to manipulate that space reflects the design idea. At the request of the director, the designer must determine the best possible relationship between positive space, the space occupied by a mass, and negative space, the unoccupied space in between. These relationships change constantly in the multiscene musical, and their creative organization into a fluid and stimulating sequence represents a primary objective for the musical theater design artist.

Line. What is a line? Any extension of a point. It can be straight or curved, combined into angles or circles, and move in any direction. It defines shapes, marks borders, conveys textures. Horizontal lines delineate the boundaries of stage floor and overhead masking; vertical lines delineate the wings, vertical maskings, and standing scenery. Straight lines suggest strength and energy. Curved lines suggest grace and femininity. Vertical lines overwhelm. Horizontal lines caress. The designer uses line within composition to give the setting a visual rhythm consistent with the interpretation of the director.

Shape. Shape occurs when line encloses space. Of particular interest to the designer is the size of the shape (height, width, depth), the relationship of one shape to another (cylinder to cube, cube to rectangle), and the relationship of all shapes to the whole. These shapes can be natural (scallop, shell, oak leaf, tulip), geometric (square, triangle, rectangle), nonspecific (blots, shards, puddles), or original.

Color. The most strikingly visible design element for the majority in the audience of a Broadway musical is color. Color can initiate visual motion, alter audience perception of form, and reverse the direction of line in a composition. To harness that considerable power, the designer must understand the primary, secondary, and tertiary divisions of color and the qualities of color like hue, value, and intensity. He may choose hot colors to stimulate, cool colors to soothe, warm colors to advance, cool colors to recede. Specific colors can then be combined into monochromatic, analogous, or complementary color schemes. While space services the movement of the show, color provokes the desired emotional and aesthetic reaction.

Texture. Texture enriches a setting by communicating to the audience a sense of how the scenery on stage must feel to the touch. Textures can be smooth, rough, lumpy, bumpy, or scratchy.

THE PRINCIPLES OF DESIGN

The principles of design which regulate these materials are harmony, balance, proportion, emphasis, and rhythm.

Harmony. A stage design is said to be harmonious when all elements cohere in a way that gives the impression of artistic unity. In a musical, each setting should be harmonious with every other and with the design concept of the show.

Balance. A balanced design distributes visual weight equally on each side of a center line. In symmetry, one side of the stage duplicates the other exactly. An irregular arrangement of elements on each side of the stage achieves asymmetry. Symmetry suggests order and formality; asymmetry suggests casual informality.

Proportion. Proportion denotes the comparative relationship between the parts of the design to each other, the entire composition, and the actor. The size of a stage form in relation to the size of a human being is called *scale.*

Emphasis. Design exercises the principle of emphasis when it directs audience attention to a focal point. Most design artists build settings around a strong center of interest with important subordinate areas. Since design for the musical theater must focus the true center of interest on the singing, moving, dancing actor, the emphasis changes constantly. Stage lighting facilitates these changes. The dimout, blackout, and crossfade on performers in different groupings allows the director to vary the stage pictures and achieve the variety of visual emphasis so characteristic of the form.

Rhythm. The relationships between forms in a design composition can communicate a sense of recurrent movement we call *rhythm.* Line accounts for the rhythm built into most designs. Repeated diagonal lines convey a sense of vigorous movement; repeated vertical or horizontal lines convey a peaceful, static quality. The creative collaboration between director and designer in the musical theater should insure harmony between design rhythm and performance rhythm. The curved and circular Boris Aronson designs for *Fiddler on the Roof* correspond to the circular concept director-choreographer Jerome Robbins built into the staging and movement of the production.

THE DESIGN FORMAT

The musical theater book with its many scenes of varying length encourages a design format that utilizes any one or combination of the following: wing and backdrop, unit set, or space stage. In the *wing-and-backdrop format,* the drops lift into the fly space above the stage as the side wings are themselves replaced. These hanging units can be curtains, borders, backdrops, scrims, screens, or cycloramas. Most multiscene Broadway musicals combine the wing-and-drop format with standing units made of flats—rectangular wooden frames covered with canvas and painted accordingly. Although the designer can use

251

The curved and circular Boris Aronson designs for *Fiddler on the Roof* reflect the circular concepts director-choreographer Jerome Robbins built into the original production. (Photo: Theatre and Music Collection, Museum of the City of New York)

flats for any type of scenery (rock formations, mountains, architectural projections), their most common application is for interior scenery. An alternative to the multiset approach is the *unit set*, a design format based on the imaginative reuse of the same scenery elements in a scheme that suggests necessary changes. When the unit set remains stationary throughout and several locales coexist on stage at the same time, the unit is called a *simultaneous scene setting*. The unit set format permits the combination of fixed and moving parts, too, as in the Boris Aronson design for *Company*. The *space stage* is an acting area defined by a pool of light. It offers the designer the most practical and modest alternative to the other formats. The space stage offers two advantages: Changes of environment can be made as quickly as a lighting crossfade, and lighting environments create the desired illusion through a direct appeal to audience imagination.

Whatever the format, the scenery in musical theater must appear to be light, spontaneous, and mobile. As the musical theater moves, so must its settings.

252

EPILOGUE

With the contemporary ballad opera *Sweeney Todd* (1979), the American musical theater has run full circle on its course of creative self-renewal. Like certain flora on the shores of the Mediterranean that send new and vigorous shoots periodically from old and venerable roots, the American musical has developed such forms in recent years as the concept musical, the rock musical, rock opera, and the hybrid revue—none of which has yet established itself as the incontestable wave of the future.

The best examples of the concept musical have come from the creative collaboration of Stephen Sondheim and Harold Prince. Here, all the elements of a musical show integrate into the whole, style and attitude considerations predominate, and the entire production develops out of an overriding theatrical idea imposed by the director. More often than not, story is reduced to a parade of dramatic vignettes or abandoned altogether. Situation replaces plot, characters appear more flat than round, and *how* the material is handled takes precedence over *what* the material says. Above all, the concept musical makes the medium the message. Undoubtedly, its most successful shows (*Company, Follies* and *A Chorus Line*) stand at the top of the American musical theater's accomplishment in the 1970s.

Whereas the rock musical burst onto the scene as the sensation of the 1960s, no shows of enduring value have been created in that mold since the initial creative surge that produced *Hair, Godspell, Your Own Thing,* **254** and *Two Gentlemen of Verona*. Perhaps the rock musical had nothing truly different to offer beyond the initial novelty of hearing rock music on the Broadway stage. While *Hair* became a tremendous international success, time and changing mores have withered away its once shocking contemporaneity. Although the rock musical regaled the public with exciting sounds that captured the spirit of the times, its theater proved all too inconsiderable. Said Frank Levy in the *Village Voice*, ". . . rock music and good lyrics by themselves don't make for good theater."* Not surprisingly, the rock opera frenzy initiated by *Tommy* and *Jesus Christ Superstar* declined simultaneously with the popularity of those productions.

The hybrid revue *(Ain't Misbehavin', Dancin')* represents too personal and derivative a treatment of material to light the path the musical will take in the 1980s. And while dance has emerged as a dominant and gratifying element in such musical shows as *Pippin, Chicago, A Chorus Line*, and the aforementioned *Dancin'*, its future in musical theater cannot be divorced from its roots in the total collaborative process. The modern musical evolved into a mature state primarily because of the primacy of the book. Since dance was never intended to exist outside its function as collaborative support, its place in the musical theater will always be tied to the book it must illustrate.

While many of the concept musicals, rock musicals, rock operas, and hybrid revues continue to play before enthusiastic audiences, no dominant body of work has yet emerged to set the course of the American musical in a direction apart from that of the Stephen Sondheim–Harold Prince collaborations. If and when that new and important phenomenon appears, as it did in the work of Jerome Kern, Rodgers and Hammerstein, and Stephen Sondheim, then the American musical theater tradition will take another giant step in its certain evolution. When that will happen, no one can predict. The final word on

* From a review of *Two Gentlemen of Verona* by Frank Levy (*The Village Voice*, August 12, 1971). Reprinted by permission.

that subject belongs to Richard Rodgers, who wrote in
Musical Stages: *

> I am often asked where I think the musical theatre is heading.
> It's one question I always try to dodge because I don't think
> it's heading anywhere until it's already been there. One night
> a show opens and suddenly there's a whole new concept. But
> it isn't the result of a trend; it's because one, two, three or more
> people sat down and sweated over an idea that somehow clicked
> and broke loose. It can be about anything and take off in any
> direction, and when it works, there's your present and your
> future.

* From *Musical Stages* by Richard Rodgers (New York: Random House, 1975).
Reprinted by permission.

INDEX

257

258

260

261